LEONARD COHEN

LEONARD COHEN

David Sheppard

THUNDER'S
MOUTH
PRESS

Published in the United States by
Thunder's Mouth Press
841 Broadway, Fourth Floor
New York, NY 10003

First published in Great Britain by Unanimous Ltd
254–258 Goswell Road, London EC1V 7RL

Series editor: John Aizlewood
Project editor: Nicola Birtwisle

Library of Congress Card Number: 99–69756

ISBN: 1–56025–270–7

Printed in Italy

1 2 3 4 5 6 7 8 9

CONTENTS

ACKNOWLEDGEMENTS

I'm indebted to John Aizlewood for inviting me to turn a decade's-worth of late nights spent with a full-bodied red and Leonard's intonings into 'research' for this book. Thanks too to Simon Majumdar for his encouragements, to Pete Astor and Paul Kenny for their different insights and, most importantly, Louise Clarke for her patience. Seriously besotted Cohenites are recommended to investigate Ira Nadel's biography *Various Positions: A Life of Leonard Cohen*, while those of a more literary bent will enjoy scouring Loranne Dorman and Clive Rawlins' tome-like *Leonard Cohen: Prophet of the Heart*. Cohen websites abound; most have something worthwhile or amusing to reveal.

ONE

THE STORY

Montreal is a city which, for all its elegant boule-
vards, polyglot colonial heritage and bilingual,
cosmopolitan charm, has always been something
of an anonymous also-ran in the premier league of urban
cultural hotbeds. When the alienated and endangered
bohemians of 1930s Paris and Berlin fled the rising tide
of Nazism, for example, it was to New York, Geneva and
London, not the undulating island city on The St. Lawrence
River, that they flew.

And while the artistic quarters of other émigré cities glowed
like intense filaments in the years leading up to World War II,
Montreal remained opaque and unerring, weathering its deeply
etched seasons of sun and snow with habitual, quiet stoicism.

It was into this ordered and immutable environment that
Leonard Norman Cohen was born on 21st September 1934.

The offspring of Nathan and Masha Cohen, Leonard and
his elder sister Esther were raised in a comfortable middle-
class home in the well-heeled Westmount district of the city.
Nathan Cohen, a second-generation Canadian Pole, was
a prominent Jewish businessman with his own clothing

manufacturing company. Having served with the Canadian Army he returned from the Great War a partial invalid – a condition which led to bouts of bed-ridden depression. He was a strict man who left the day-to-day running of family matters to his wife. He would always be a distant figure to his children.

Despite his poor health, the clothing business was thriving and the Cohen family was opulent enough to live in a sturdy semi-detached brick house backing on to leafy Murray Hill Park with commanding views of the river beyond. The Cohens employed a brace of servants and a chauffeur, while the children spent much of the day in the company of a nanny. Cohen *père*, whose own father was a revered rabbi and ran a profitable St. Lawrence River dredging fleet, nevertheless yearned for greater things, and took to his grave a sense of regret and frustration in his lack of upward progress on the local jewry's hierarchical ladder.

Montreal was home to a large and flourishing Jewish community and the Cohens were active within it, observing the Sabbath and attending synagogue on a regular basis – though theirs was a passive, unfanatical approach to the faith. Indeed, the young Leonard Cohen often accompanied his Irish nanny, Mary, on her visits to one or other of the district's several Catholic churches. It was the start of a lifetime's fascination with the varying manifestations of religious belief.

Masha Cohen was of Russian extraction and had emigrated to Canada with her family from their native Lithuania. She had an ear for music and was given to renderings of obscure Russian folk laments essayed in a lugubrious, heavily accented contralto. Her by turns melancholic and romantic temperament – not to mention her vocal characteristics – were destined to re-appear in their only son, alongside elements of her husband's prim sobriety.

A bright, even studious boy, the young Cohen attended Roslyn Junior School, a few minutes' walk from the family domicile, where he showed an early aptitude for music, combining arduous piano lessons with playground reveries on a penny whistle and stints on the clarinet in the school band. His mother encouraged these ventures with some vigour, repeatedly advising him to 'follow your little heart'.

Nathan Cohen died prematurely at the age of 52, when Leonard was nine years old. The event had a profound effect on the young schoolboy – a psychological scar that was to influence and characterise much of the writer's nascent outpourings. To this day he cites events around the time of his father's death as emblematic of his abiding artistic preoccupations.

One typically symbolic act was to conceal a scrap of paper on which he'd composed some poetic lines in the folds of his late father's bow tie, which he then proceeded to bury with solemn ritual in the back garden. 'I've been digging in the garden for years, looking for it,' Cohen once admitted with typically enigmatic metaphorical intent, 'maybe that's all I'm doing, looking for the note.'

His school years unfurled without seismic event. An early interest in chemistry soon gave way to a burgeoning penchant for literature, and with it a mushrooming interest in his Jewish heritage in general and the Holocaust in particular.

His father had been an enthusiastic reader, and although his tastes ran more to the prosaic articles in the *Reader's Digest* than to the bound volumes of Chaucer, Milton and Longfellow that lined his study shelves, the influence of his bookishness, however ersatz, was keenly felt by his son.

Cohen attended Westmount High School and simultaneously took his place at Hebrew *shul*, ostensibly to be in the company of his maternal grandfather, another rabbi – he was still grieving heavily for his father – but also, via the pages of the Old Testament, to indulge his new-found appetite for the written word. He was particularly taken with the book of Isaiah and its grandiloquently expressed themes of loss and redemption, although in truth the poetry of the English translation, rather than the more archaic Hebrew, is what truly excited him.

Similarly, his secular studies found their focus in the English Literature department at Westmount High, where he soon became something of a star scholar. Back in his father's study, the classic tomes began to be dusted off.

During the summer of 1949, Cohen wandered into one of Montreal's second-hand bookshops for what was becoming a habitual browse, and happened upon a slim volume of poems by Federico Garcia Lorca. Discovering Lorca was a rite of passage more personal and profound than the bar mitzvah ceremony he had undertaken two years previously. 'Lorca ruined my life!,' he was later to expostulate, alluding ironically to the Spanish poet's inestimable impact on the young bibliophile. In Lorca Cohen found a voice that spoke directly to him as no other had. Here was writing of coruscating passion, a piquant meeting of the sacred and profane, the Book of Isaiah shorn of moral worthiness and soaked in achingly fecund surrealistic images. At the tender age of 15, Leonard Cohen had found his métier, and he began writing poetry in earnest.

His cravings for the muse often took him for solitary walks in the park that lay behind the family home. On one such amble he encountered a young Hispanic boy gently strumming a guitar. It was a gut-strung Spanish instrument, the type with which Cohen would later become synonymous.

Fascinated, he soon struck up a friendship with the youngster and in no time was receiving lessons in rudimentary finger picking and chord shaping. Trying to contact the youth by phone one day soon afterwards, Cohen was dumbfounded to learn that his new compadre had hung himself. Another sacramental death had cast its shadow across the fledgling *poète maudit's* path.

Cohen graduated from Westmount High in 1951 and enrolled at Montreal's prestigious McGill University to study Arts the following autumn. He kept on with the guitar in the time allowed by his voracious thirst for poetry and a new-found, if somewhat less cerebral passion: girls.

A friend's magician father, coupled with the discovery of a somewhat dubious Victorian manual on the subject led Cohen to a brief dalliance with hypnotism, during which he managed to put the family maid under his mesmeric spell. The stripling voyeur used the opportunity to remove the girl's clothes, only to find he was unable to return her to consciousness. In the end he had to slap her to bring her round and make his excuses as best he could. The incident would later be recounted – with slight embellishments – in Cohen's first novel, *The Favourite Game*.

His sexual proclivities also manifested themselves in a series of paramours increasingly drawn to his broodingly enigmatic presence as staid Westmount's young bohemian-in-residence. A litany of brief romantic encounters and priapic fumblings culminated in a serious relationship with a 17-year-old artist named Freda Guttman. She was the first of many female muses whose intimate involvement with Cohen would provide lyrical inspiration. Their affair ebbed and flowed for four years, during which time his stock as a poet, not to mention his sap, would begin to rise.

In the meantime, music was asserting itself amid an ever more frenetic schedule. In the summer of 1951 he formed The Buckskin Boys, a basic-sounding three-piece featuring Cohen on guitar and two college pals on broomstick bass and harmonica. Their name derived from a shared penchant for cowboy-style suede jackets, wearing which they played skeletal versions of the country and western standards of the day at college dances and church basement youth clubs. Cohen had developed a taste for country music picked up from radio stations powerfully beamed from the southern states of the USA. He had also begun to acquire a collection of new-fangled long-playing records. Hank Williams was a particular favourite.

Cohen's time at McGill was character-building rather than academically meteoric. He was an active and precociously erudite member of the Debating Union and popular with his fellow students, but, despite winning prizes for literature, he sleepwalked his way through most of the curriculum, spending much of his time off-campus in the company of fellow students Mort Rosengarten and Robert Hershorn (both friends from schooldays), with whom he formed a tight-knit gang. All the same, his abilities with voice and guitar, although still rough-hewn, made him a focal point at campus parties, while a prodigious propensity for alcohol led to his gaining something of a reputation as an uninhibited bon viveur. 'I'll drink out of anything that has a bottom to it,' he was reported to have commented at the time.

His thoughts about a choice of career during his college years vacillated between the law, academia, music and his father's clothing business, although all the while it was poetry that tugged at his consciousness most acutely. While his literature studies returned him happily enough to Lorca, there were new discoveries – notably Yeats, Eliot and Rimbaud – to partially sate an increasingly ravenous appetite for poetry.

Most significant was the fact that McGill's English department contained a cadre of notable Canadian literary eminences, all of whom were to exert a positive influence on Cohen. The novelist Hugh MacLennan and the poet Louis Dudek gave valuable support and advice to their patently gifted teenage charge, though it was the catalytic role played by the poet and pedagogue Irving Layton that had the most acute effect on Cohen's growth as a writer.

Layton was the *enfant terrible* of the 1950s Canadian literary scene. Charismatic and opinionated, his poetry, like his character, was visceral, volatile and full of wit. Layton and Cohen immediately formed a bond which took a form less as teacher and pupil and more as kindred rebel poets. It speaks volumes for Cohen's precipitous talents that Layton saw their relationship strictly in these terms. 'Leonard was already a genius when we met,' was his subsequent unequivocal claim. Cohen was impressed by Layton's prolific output and belief in the potency of poetry. The older man also represented a respected patriarchal figure for the fatherless Cohen – there would be others in the years to come – and to this day the two remain firm friends.

Spurred on by Layton and still-girlfriend Freda Guttman, Cohen began circulating his poems to the appropriate magazines. His first published work was titled 'A Halloween Poem To Delight My Younger Friends', which appeared in a literary quarterly named *CIV/n* (after Ezra Pound's abbreviation for the word *civilization*) and there followed a sheaf of submissions to the magazine's later issues, as well as to the student magazine *Forge*. Cohen's first book of poems was published after graduating with a barely serviceable degree from McGill in 1955.

Let Us Compare Mythologies, dedicated to the memory of his father, was the first title to appear in the newly created McGill Poetry series, with accompanying line drawings by Guttman. Comprising the cream of Cohen's teenage oeuvre, the 44 collected poems were printed in an edition of 500, which duly sold out, aided by his own entrepreneurial élan. Cohen distributed the text to local bookshops himself, and even placed an advertisement in the college newspaper. The wordsmith's career had begun in earnest.

Around this time Cohen began publicly reciting (it could hardly yet be called performing) his works, often accompanied by a jazz pianist. He held forth in places such as the grandly titled Birdland club (essentially just a room above a downtown Montreal steakhouse) and at various campus venues. Recorded examples of his almost incongruously zestful readings of the era appeared on the album *Six Montreal Poets*. Irving Layton and Louis Dudek contributed to the same disc.

In the autumn of 1956, as rock 'n' roll's *tsunami* was breaking all over North America in the wake of Elvis Presley, Leonard Cohen abandoned putative plans to study law and headed south to New York. A post-graduate year at Columbia University would provide him with not only the cachet of a diploma from a prestigious American seat of learning, but also, crucially, some time to think and write. This was important because, having eschewed the possibility of a legal career, he was yet to decide upon a suitably money-garnering vocation. Poetry didn't seem likely to figure in any such pecuniary prognoses. He had already earned some vital dollars between college semesters at his uncle's brass works and in the Cohens' clothing factory but, despite finding himself something of a dab hand with the sewing machine, the published poet-graduate found such menial roles held only a limited appeal.

Once at Columbia, putting aside the apparently unavoidable fact that a life in art and one in the black were destined to be mutual exclusives, he set about exploring the creative well-spring that was contemporary Manhattan. This was only aided by his distaste for Columbia's post-graduate school, which he found uninspiring and dispiriting, applying himself to his studies with even more indolence than he had at McGill.

Naturally gravitating to the bohemian epicentre of Greenwich Village, Cohen mingled with marginal elements of the Beat poet crowd then packing out every coffee-house worth its cappuccino froth within spitting distance of Washington Square. It was a scene apparently made for an occasionally beret-sporting, poet tyro like Cohen.

Here was mystical, be-bop verse looming large over the cultural stage, espoused by a wild, hip and rebellious group bent on setting about the American literary establishment with an amphetamine-dipped pen. Allen Ginsberg's epochal *Howl* was published during Cohen's Manhattan sojourn, and the seismic shift in popular cultural mores occurring at that time was palpable to as sensitive a man as Cohen.

It was the dawn of the beatnik era, which was perhaps the earliest incident of parent-worrying youth tribalism. Given its tendency toward poetry-spouting, jazz-digging, and marijuana-smoking, Cohen should have taken to the scene like the proverbial duck to water (he had already been introduced to the delights of pot and peyote back in Montreal) – superficially at least, he was beatnik *in excelsis*.

He was certainly impressed by witnessing a rumbustious

Jack Kerouac poetry reading-cum-performance that was bolstered by the carcenings of a febrile be-bop combo and fuelled by torrents of bourbon. Kerouac's seminal novel *On The Road* would be published the next year. Conspicuously – and not wholly uncoincidentally – Cohen's ardour for poetry was, if not cooling, then at least being threatened by and made to share page room with explorative prose writing and the formative sketches for a novel.

But despite the various serendipities, Cohen felt more comfortable, in New York at least, as the singular outsider and, even among so many like minds, couldn't quite find it within himself to join the counter-culture party. 'I liked the places they gathered,' he has said of his brief exposure to the downtown New York scene, 'but I was never accepted by the bohemians. I was too middle-class, I didn't have the right credentials.'

Female assignations, needless to say, did play a prominent part in Cohen's New York life. Most significant was a brief liaison with a free-thinking, dark-haired beauty named Anne Sherman, a fellow Columbia student. Two years Cohen's senior, she rapidly became his latest muse and the inspiration for much of the poetry he would subsequently write (most of which ended up in 1961's *The Spice-Box Of Earth*) and would later appear as a character in his slowly germinating novel.

Though outwardly conservative, Sherman was a willing fellow-traveller on Cohen's lengthening sexual odyssey and despite the affair lasting only a few months, Cohen would often express his affection for her in the years to come.

Cohen stayed less than a year at Columbia all told, before returning to Montreal and a further litany of day jobs. When not out carousing with women in the company of his sculptor friend from McGill days Mort Rosengarten, he busied his work-free hours with poetry and rented a small downtown apartment – much to his over-protective mother's chagrin – ostensibly as a writing den. He even got as far as publishing one issue of a highbrow-meets-Beat-style literary magazine called *The Phoenix* ('We want experiment, we want controversy,' he wrote in his opening editorial) and helped run a downtown art gallery before a fire put paid to that enterprise.

In the solitude of the apartment, Cohen beavered away at his typewriter with the care and rigour that is the hallmark of his creative regime to this day. At the same time he gave his first professional poetry readings around Montreal coffee-houses and – often accompanied by a 12-piece ensemble – in more established venues such as the subterranean Dunn's Progressive Jazz Parlour. He was beginning to draw an audience, for his mordant wit and declamatory style made him an entertaining raconteur, the relative merits of his verse notwithstanding.

He was also addressing himself yet again to the thorny problem of a career, hitting on some quixotic, short-lived plans to forge an alternative working life. First he applied to the Hong Kong police force but was turned down without explanation (although he was theoretically suitable insofar as he was a Commonwealth citizen). Then, several attempts to become a teacher of English in India fizzled out.

The summer of 1958 dragged on with Cohen writing poetry, pondering his novel and working as a counsellor at Pripstein's youth summer camp north of Montreal. Apart from blessing his boisterous adolescent wards with the wisdom of all his 24 years and his by now dextrous guitar playing, the ever-libidinous Cohen spent much of the season pursuing women. These included an American art counsellor and even the camp nurse, who become the inspiration for one of his most celebrated early poems, 'As The Mist Leaves No Scar', later re-written as 'True Love Leaves No Traces' on the *Death Of A Ladies' Man* LP.

At the end of the summer, Cohen found himself once again confronting the familiar art-versus-a-profession impasse. Art found its outlet in a finished collection of poetry Cohen christened *The Spice-Box Of Earth*, which he sent to the Canadian publisher McClelland & Stewart in Toronto. To Cohen's immense satisfaction Jack McClelland, then one of Canada's most prominent literary figures, agreed to publish the work, given certain amendments, including reducing the quota of erotic verse. It was eventually published in the spring of 1961.

As for a profession, salvation, or at least a stay of execution, came by way of an arts scholarship from The Canada Council which furnished him with the tidy sum of $3,000. Without romantic ties and with a brief bout of play-writing with Irving Layton resulting only in demoralising rejection slips, Cohen took the money as a travel purse and headed, in December 1959, for London.

It was not strictly a case of vacation before vocation, for Cohen chose London as the ideal city of exile in which to work on the novel he had been readying since returning from graduate school. It was not strictly his first. He had written a short work of fiction entitled *A Ballet Of Lepers* in the months before leaving for Columbia, in which his dark musings on the Jewish Holocaust had been given a melodramatic airing. The few manuscripts he sent out met only with polite refusal.

London at the end of the 1950s was a dour place for a young man who had already enjoyed the relative exotica of New

York in its pomp, but Cohen had romantic illusions about penning a great work in the land of Shakespeare and the then *au courant* 'angry young' writers typified by playwright John Osborne.

He berthed in Hampstead, an affluent suburb of North London, at the home of Jake and Stella Pullman – old friends of Mort Rosengarten's parents, who were assiduous in encouraging Cohen to write (the story goes that Stella Pullman wouldn't let him out of the house unless he had completed a daily output of three close-typed pages).

In London, Cohen purchased the green Olivetti 22 typewriter that stayed with him for the next 30 years, and, from Burberry's Of Piccadilly, the 'famous blue' raincoat that would itself see 10 years' service before being stolen from a New York loft and which would become immortalised in the eponymous song.

He needed the coat. The English winter of 1959–1960 was a bleak one, even for a son of icy Quebec, and Cohen found badly heated London alienating and dreary. He even sought escape in a trip to Dublin to sample W.B. Yeats's old drinking haunts. He would later find London's nightlife more stimulating – particularly relishing West Indian 'blues' parties and their reliable bushels of premium marijuana.

None the less, the keenly gregarious Cohen made friends in London. Among them were Jacob Rothschild – later Lord Rothschild – to whom he was introduced by a Canadian acquaintance named Tony Graham. But the majority of his time was taken up with writing. By March 1960 he'd completed the first draft of his book, then titled *Beauty At Close Quarters* and later published as *The Favourite Game*, and began to plot his next move.

The novel was deeply autobiographical, centring on the

exploits of one Lawrence Breavman, born in Montreal in September 1934. Many of his friends and adolescent adventures were immortalised in fictional form within its pages. He didn't even bother to change some of the names. True to Cohen's own family background, Breavman's businessman father appears as an invalid, and his mother as an overbearing Jewish stereotype.

Cohen felt duly proud of the work and of having finished it in less than four months. A friend from Montreal, Nancy Becall, who was also staying with the Pullmans, read the draft and later declared it a far greater work than the eventually published re-write.

Ever the industrious and disciplined worker, Cohen then set about amending the final version of *The Spice-Box Of Earth*, although his impatience with the verse form was made clear in a letter to a friend: 'I'm glad the book is out of my hands. Poetry is so damned self-indulgent.'

One rain-sodden afternoon in March 1960, having visited a dentist in the East End in order to have a troublesome wisdom tooth attended to, Cohen found himself wandering in an aimless fashion along Bank Street. Stepping out of the rain into the welcoming portals of the Bank Of Greece, he began to chat with a suntanned teller, bronzed from a recent trip to the Aegean.

His itinerant instincts aroused and, business in London apparently at a point of conclusion, Cohen sought out a travel agent and immediately booked himself a one-way ticket to Athens.

Arriving in the Greek capital in early April, he swiftly set about booking his steamer passage to the island of Hydra. He chose the tiny Aegean island partially on the recommendation of his new friend Jacob Rothschild, whose mother had married a Greek painter whose family owned an impressive mansion on the island.

Hydra was also something of a bohemian colony, its reputation for cheap, easy living going before it. Cohen was perhaps aware of Henry Miller's observation that Hydra was a place of 'wild and naked perfection'. Certainly such a seemingly romantic geographic idyll would have appealed incalculably to Cohen who, having found Montreal restrictive, New York frenetic and London coldly dispiriting, was yearning for an inspirational locale.

Rooming initially at the house of the Australian journalist George Johnston, Cohen was quickly, predictably, smitten with the place. The Aegean spring was warm and welcoming and he found the expatriate cabal of writers and artists entirely to his taste. He struck up a friendship with the English painter Anthony Kingsmill and made the acquaintance of several other writers such as William Lederer, Paul Desmond and the Norwegian novelist Axel Jensen, all of whom made nightly visits to the tiny harbour-side bar that was the island's social hub.

But Cohen's most important conquest on Hydra was Marianne Ihlen – Axel Jensen's Norwegian girlfriend.

A striking blonde, Marianne had been a successful international model and was now preoccupied with bringing up a young son – also called Axel – while living out the death-throes of a doomed relationship with Jensen.

With its retinue of dislocated arty types and rudderless bon viveurs, Hydra at the turn of the '60s was a hotbed of sexual intrigue, the coterie mired in a labyrinth of incestuous affairs. Cohen, naturally enough, felt right at home.

He fell for Marianne with unbridled ardour and when Jensen left the island with his latest flame in tow, he wasted no time in wooing her. Marianne in turn was charmed by Cohen's generous spirit and old-world eloquence. They soon became lovers and when, in September 1960, Cohen purchased (for the princely sum of $1,500) a white-washed house overlooking the bay, she and young Axel moved in. Cohen was *en famille* once more.

Even more so than those who had gone before her, Marianne proved a prodigiously fertile source of inspiration for Cohen and a companion whose gentle, bordering-on-servile nature complemented her willowy presence. Cohen even discovered previously latent paternal instincts (he knew, after all, what it was to be fatherless) and doted on little Axel.

To counterweight the domestic stability, Cohen found himself increasingly drawn to the variety of drugs that were available on the island. Hashish was widely used on Hydra and Cohen more than dabbled with it, later going on to experiment with opium and amphetamines. Although he used narcotics principally to enhance his literary imagination (he thought himself the inheritor of a tradition of artificially aided creativity stretching back to Rimbaud and De Quincey) his escalating reliance on various stimulants caused Marianne concern. Tellingly, Cohen remarked in a contemporary letter that there was 'nothing sadder than an empty opium drawer'. He was later to decry his use of amphetamines as a catalyst for writing: 'It [speed] isn't a very good drug for depressed people because coming down is very bad. It took me 10 years to recover.'

When domestic bliss turned, with grim inevitability, to claustrophobia, Cohen packed his bags and returned, at the end of 1960, to Montreal. It was a pattern that was to be repeated throughout his life: self-imposed exile followed by repentant return.

His impatience with life on Hydra was only exacerbated by Jack McClelland's negative response to the first draft of *Beauty At Close Quarters*. McClelland thought the novel, although beautifully written, was too autobiographical and self-indulgent to engage as a work of fiction. Duly chastened, Cohen began to re-immerse himself in the Canadian literary life. He also made serious attempts to drum up renewed interest in his book. Publishers Secker & Warburg made him an offer which he considered for some time whilst pondering a rewrite.

His wanderlust once more activated by a brief respite in familiar surroundings, Cohen was soon off on his travels again. This time he chose Cuba as the place to re-fire his engines. It was a contentious choice.

Cuba in 1961 was in the throes of a diplomatic stand-off between Castro's two-year-old Communist government and the itchy trigger finger of the USA. Indeed, the anxious eyes of the world were focusing on the northern Caribbean. A CIA-backed invasion was expected at any day and in April an abortive attempt took place at The Bay Of Pigs which came close to starting an all-out conflict between the superpowers.

Cohen, with typically romantic braggadocio, entered into proceedings without trepidation. His motivations were fanciful rather than political, for he was all too aware that he was following in Lorca's footsteps, the Spanish poet having sampled and adored Havana life back in the 1920s when things were very different. It was a dubious enterprise, as Cohen later admitted: 'I thought maybe this was my Spanish Civil War.'

Nevertheless Cohen spent his time carousing in Havana's still exotic backstreet bars and took to sporting military fatigues and a rough beard in the style made popular by local folk hero Ernesto 'Che' Guevara. Ironically, it was in this guise that he was mistakenly arrested shortly after the Bay Of Pigs emergency, his captors initially convinced that he was the leader of another invasion attempt.

Cohen left Cuba, not without some bureaucratic difficulty, in late April and returned once more to Montreal. In May, *The Spice-Box Of Earth* was published to general adulation. Cohen's star was beginning to rise. Partly as a result, The Canada Council renewed his bursary, and with it Cohen returned to Greece and to Marianne.

Here he worked on revisions for his novel – now retitled *The Favourite Game* – and returned to the lotus-eating expatriate's lifestyle. He also fixed up a first floor room of his five-storey house as a music room, complete with Spanish guitar, Dansette and albums.

In March 1962 he was back in London at the Pullmans', with the aim of finishing the second draft of *The Favourite Game* away from the sexual, climatic and drug-related distractions of Hydra. Here, ironically, he reacquainted himself with the aromatic sensimilla of the city's West Indian neighbourhoods and became, incongruously, a disciple of the Twist.

In November, after a short stint back on Hydra, Cohen found himself in Paris at the behest of The Canadian Broadcasting Company to record a radio programme on the subject of Crisis In Western Culture. On the panel with him were such luminaries as the eminent English writer/theologian Malcolm Muggeridge and distinguished novelist Mary McCarthy. The articulate and charming Cohen more than held his own with the illustrious pair.

After Paris it was on to New York where *The Favourite Game* was finally to be published by Viking, but only after

Cohen had made countless alterations to the original text.

He was soon at work on a new clutch of darkly themed poems (most of which would later be published as *Flowers For Hitler*) and undertook a reading tour of Canada, where he was rapidly assuming the mantle of household name.

Perhaps as a result of so much time away, his relationship with Marianne entered a new, rocky phase. She had busied herself modelling for an island boutique and attending to Axel while Cohen's attentions were monopolised by his writings and by entertaining his male friends. For, despite the turmoil of a relationship in crisis, Cohen's house remained open to an almost constant stream of visitors attracted to the increasingly well-known lassitude afforded by Hydra and to his own new-found celebrity status.

Novelists, painters and folk singers sought him out with an alarming regularity, as did various peripatetic women, on one or other leg of a 1960s version of the Grand Tour. They were drawn to Cohen's *soi-disant* bohemian aura, much as the impressionable teenage girls of Westmount had been. Marianne's tolerance bordered on the saintly.

In the autumn of 1962 Cohen was once again in Canada, this time to attend a literary festival in eastern Quebec, where he stole the show, despite being in the company of the great and the good of the Canadian literary scene.

During an extended stop-over in Montreal he made the acquaintance of a woman named Suzanne Verdal, an artist and dancer who captivated the poet whilst performing a choreographed routine with her husband in a downtown club. Although apparently they were never lovers, Cohen did share several long, candle-lit nights in Suzanne's Montreal loft where they, allegedly, did little more than discuss art. Suzanne was soon the subject of several Cohen poems (two of them were published in his 1966 *Parasites of Heaven* collection) and one of which would later transmute into his signature song 'Suzanne'.

In December of 1963 Cohen addressed a symposium on the future of Judaism in Canada. He was a figure of some standing now and used the opportunity to express some contentious views about, as he saw it, the Jewish community's overweening allegiance to commerce and its neglect of its artistic heritage and of contemporary Jewish artists.

For a while Cohen became a focus of controversy in Canadian public life, which of course only added to the clamour to see him when he began a highly successful and remunerative trans-Canadian reading tour in early 1964.

Ego and wallet duly refurbished, Cohen jetted back to the Aegean bursting with renewed enthusiasm for the written word. On his return he set up a writing area on his sun terrace and, with portable record-player disgorging the choice tones of Ray Charles, set about blackening pages for a new novel. It already had a title: *Beautiful Losers*.

With only one hiatus (in Canada later in the year to pick up the $4,000 Prix Literature Du Quebec, awarded to him for *The Favourite Game*), Cohen devoted his time to *Beautiful Losers* with a steely determination.

During the autumn stint back home Cohen undertook another lengthy reading tour, this time organised by Jack McClelland. In the company of various other poets including old mentor Irving Layton, Cohen capitalised on his increasingly lofty status – he rarely failed to pack a hall – which, although time-consuming, bought him more novel-writing time back on Hydra. Much of the tour was captured on film by Donald Brittain – some of it appearing in his 1965 documentary *Ladies & Gentlemen...Mr. Leonard Cohen*.

Beautiful Losers eschewed the naked autobiographical slant of its predecessor and found Cohen in expansive mood, dwelling on politics and history with a nod to Eastern mysticism here and to native North American mythology there. As usual, existential *longueurs* and dissections of sexual practice were the major concerns. Combining a variety of narrative devices, Cohen ranged over his chosen topics, skipping from advertising jargon and hipster-speak one minute to journalese and arcane language the next. Popping copious amounts of amphetamines and fasting to improve his concentration, by late 1965 the first draft was complete.

Despite its obvious qualities Jack McClelland was still dubious about publishing Cohen's fiction – there were several re-writes before he was content to go ahead – but at the end of March 1966 Cohen's opus was finally unleashed on the Canadian public.

Reviews were generally unfavourable – again the erotic quotient was too high and perhaps too arbitrary-seeming for most – but Cohen pronounced himself satisfied: 'It's the best thing I've ever done,' was his unconstrained verdict.

But despite his sanguine mood, an old problem was still gnawing away at Cohen's peace of mind. His books were selling in the hundreds rather than the thousands, and what little advances he had been able to wring out of his publishers had been just enough to sustain the writer's life in Greece, but no more. A final poetry collection, *Parasites Of Heaven*, was published later in 1966; again the reviews were no more than lukewarm.

His thoughts turned to journalism after he had been approached by the CBC to present a current affairs programme, although this eventually came to nothing. Slowly he found himself tiring of the exiled writer's life and began to yearn to be at the centre of things again. Simultaneously he began to embrace his musical calling, one that, in suppressed form, had accompanied him throughout most of his 32 years. At least in this direction the writer's path forward might be strewn with dollars.

Cohen had been using music in his poetry readings for some years – generally a jazz-based combo of one type or other – and music had been the constant accompaniment to his bouts of intense novel-writing during the last year. He later argued that he had always thought of his poems as songs. Now he would prove it. With indecent, almost panic-stricken, urgency he threw himself, to the exclusion of all else, into songwriting.

Around him popular music was exploding into an unprecedented cultural phenomenon. The Beatles ruled half the world's airwaves and monopolised the media (it was the year of John Lennon's outburst about his group being 'bigger than Jesus'). The Rolling Stones were putting a razor-sharp winkle-picker to Tin Pan Alley's genteel facade and, most significantly for Cohen, Bob Dylan was releasing his *Blonde On Blonde* masterpiece which fused coruscating surrealistic language with shimmering electro-acoustic rock music.

Cohen had been following Dylan's career with some interest – unsurprisingly since both the accolades and brickbats Dylan was receiving (visionary artist and spokesman for a generation on one hand, pseudo-poet and self-indulgent Romantic on the other), echoed exactly those meted out to Cohen.

With Dylan's meteoric rise very much at the front of his mind, Cohen decided to throw in his lot with the music scene, and moved, in October 1966, to its beating American heart, New York City. Although initially unaware of the prodigious elevation of folk music from esoteric marginalisation to the pop mainstream (in the afterglow of Dylan's trailblazing – despite his eschewing of the form in favour of electric rock 'n' roll), Cohen's cultural antennae were as perceptive as ever.

Within weeks he had holed up in The Chelsea hotel on West 23rd Street, once the domicile of Dylan Thomas, William Burroughs, Arthur Miller and, most recently, Bob Dylan. With its crumbling Edwardian grandeur and labyrinth of eccentrically decorated, low-rent rooms, the Chelsea was the bohemian nexus of contemporary New York counter-cultural life. Cohen had found the perfect base from which to launch his assault on the ears of America.

An oft-documented 1967 chance meeting with singer Janis Joplin in the Chelsea's creaky elevator found its way into another Cohen signature song: 'Chelsea Hotel', a not atypical instance of the artist interaction that took place within the building's privacy-insuring, three-feet thick walls.

Cohen began returning to his old haunts in the West Village. Where he had once mingled with the Beat crowd, he now rubbed shoulders with folk hipsters and proto-hippies in clubs like The Bitter End and The Copper Kettle. But although he yearned to join the party, his initial attempts to interest agents and managers in his singer-songwriting abilities fell on unresponsive ears.

One reason was that, at 32, he was perceived to be too old. Dylan was seven years his junior and Cohen, who had always looked older than his years, had the double disadvantage of having to disavow a 15-year career as a writer before he could enter the circle then being staked out by guitar-strumming luminaries like Joan Baez, Judy Collins, Phil Ochs and David Blue. While Cohen explored the downtown zeitgeist, Marianne and Axel, who had followed Cohen from Greece, were installed in a Lower East Side loft, thus affording Cohen the romance of the loner's solitude with the comfort of the family bosom close at hand, a typically Cohenesque paradox.

While Marianne's endurance continued, Cohen fell in love and lust as regularly as ever. One target of his febrile affections was the singer Nico, another Chelsea resident, then serving time as eerie Teutonic chanteuse with The Velvet Underground. Unusually, Cohen's unambiguous advances got him nowhere – Nico protested that she liked younger men (she was also then working with the teenage Jackson Browne) – but via her, Cohen was introduced to Andy Warhol and the activities of his infamous Factory arts laboratory. New York's creative fertility reinforced Cohen's desire for a taste of the action.

He befriended Velvet Underground leader Lou Reed at around the same time – the latter announcing himself a fan of Cohen's novels – and began to make further inroads into the Manhattan music scene. Most fortuitously, Cohen was introduced to Mary Martin, an associate of Albert Grossman, Bob Dylan's high-powered manager.

Cohen played his songs for Martin. He had by now completed 'Suzanne' and 'Take This Longing' (the latter written for Nico) and she was impressed enough by the songs – if not his abilities to perform them – to arrange a meeting with Judy Collins, then in the process of harvesting material for an upcoming LP.

Collins was to prove an acuitous interlocutor for and interpreter of Cohen's material. Her *In My Life* album, released at the end of 1966, included a plaintive version of 'Suzanne' while her next, *Wildflower*, released the following spring, contained a trio of Cohen originals. It was also the album that launched Collins as a pop star, containing as it did her international hit 'Both Sides Now'. Thus, Cohen found his way into the sitting rooms of the record-buying world and his hymnal songs: 'Sisters Of Mercy', 'Hey That's No Way To Say Goodbye' and 'Priests' announced the presence of a unique songwriting talent.

From poet to troubadour was not such a transition for a writer who had been performing with musical backing of one kind or another for nearly 10 years and for whom music had always exerted an influence. But not since college days at McGill and the ersatz country intonings of The Buckskin Boys had Cohen ventured onto a stage to sing before an audience. It was Judy Collins who invited Cohen back into the limelight.

On 30th April 1967 Collins was playing an anti-Vietnam war benefit at New York's Town Hall and, mid-set, the singer announced a guest appearance: Leonard Cohen. Ambling to the microphone ashen-faced, Cohen began to strum the opening bars of 'Suzanne', then stopped. His guitar was out of tune, and stage fright had reduced his voice to a nervous whimper. He walked off after a minute. Collins met him in the wings and insisted he try again. The crowd too showed their support, willing Cohen back with the vehemence usually reserved for a hard-won encore. Cohen duly responded and went back to finish his song.

With Collins's endorsement, his profile as a performer as well as writer of songs was now sufficiently enhanced for Cohen to find himself the object of much speculative enquiry from the same A&R fraternity who had dismissed his earlier advances. Most notable amongst these was John Hammond, Columbia Records' principal talent scout. It was Hammond who had signed Billie Holiday to the label and had similarly taken a risk on the young, unknown Bob Dylan, much to the bemusement of his colleagues who had christened the scruffy Woody Guthrie manqué 'Hammond's Folly'.

Hammond clearly saw potential for Dylan-like success with Leonard Cohen, and there was certainly room for more than one *refusenik* Jewish folk-poet on the CBS roster. But as with Dylan, Cohen's commercial potential was underestimated by most of Hammond's A&R colleagues. Nevertheless Hammond signed Cohen to Columbia in the summer of 1967 and quickly set about arranging recording dates for a debut album.

Recorded in New York during late summer, *Songs Of Leonard Cohen* was released, oddly enough, on Boxing Day 1967. The studio had been fascinating to Cohen as he'd never even visited one before cutting the album, and he was daunted by the retinue of top-flight musicians Hammond had drafted in for the sessions. Despite being somewhat overawed, Cohen's artistic sensibilities soon took over the proceedings. He insisted on performing by the dim light of candles and on one occasion in front of a mirror (to remind him of childhood mock performances in front of the bedroom wardrobe version back in Westmount).

Cohen had a torrid relationship with producer John Simon (Janis Joplin's producer, later to gain fame as the sound engineer and so-called sixth member of The Band) who was drafted in after Hammond was taken ill and could no longer oversee the recordings. Simon's attempts to ameliorate Cohen's dirge-like minor key songs with pretty piano counterpoints and cascading strings proved to be sticking points. In the end a compromise was reached, with many of the arrangements left in, although placed, at Cohen's insistence, low in the mix, with other sounds, particularly the twanging Jew's harp (inspired by Ennio Morricone's use of the instrument on spaghetti western soundtracks of the era) mixed high.

An American chart peak of number 162 did little to convince John Hammond's more cynical workmates that CBS had the new Dylan on their books but the album fared much better in Europe, and particularly in Britain, where it reached Number 13.

Initial reviews set the standard by which Cohen's critical reaction would be gauged in years to come. Words like 'depressing', 'despairing' and 'long-suffering' infused the reviewers' purple prose from the London *Times* to *The New York Times*. The words 'Leonard Cohen' as synonyms for overwrought, bohemian melancholia were thus etched indelibly into the public consciousness.

At the same time Cohen's name began to be associated with Dylan's in the critics' lexicon. Here were two purveyors of musical gravitas, both, it seemed, trying to cut a serious swathe through an era confused by political agitation on one hand and permissive hedonism on the other. Cohen's brooding, shadowy shtick was hardly the stuff of the Summer Of Love, but his soul-searching, gypsy troubadour public image struck a chord with the burgeoning counterculture; an almost academically rigorous counterpoint to the lysergic excesses of the psychedelic revolution. Cohen was the credible antidote to hippy insouciance, the miserable-sounding sage at the tripped-out party.

Cohen promoted his debut long-player with performances on Canadian television (where he was now a genuine home-grown star) and for the BBC in London. His stage nerves now overcome, he also undertook a short promotional tour performing at several American universities and at the Newport Folk Festival. Here he met fellow Canuck Joni Mitchell, then beginning her own career on the artier margins of the folk corpus, and the two became briefly involved.

Cohen was an inspiration for Mitchell and Cohen clearly related to the singer's poetic leanings and Romantic predisposition. He followed her to the home she had just purchased in Los Angeles and spent a month living with her in the autumn of 1968.

This, coupled with a continuing litany of usually short romantic dalliances, convinced Cohen that his relationship with Marianne, already in a state of fractured suspension, should come to an end. Loyal to the last, Marianne sought yet another compromise, but she can hardly have found much comfort in her waning lover's inclusion of the hard-to-misinterpret 'So Long Marianne' on his debut album.

Prior to the album's release, Cohen, in tandem with Mary Martin, set up his own publishing company, Stranger Music. Although showing great business acumen for what was still an era of tenuous copyright rules and managerial sharp practice, Cohen nonetheless managed to walk naively into the most transparent of contractual traps. With the album in the can he signed over the rights to three of its principal songs (including the signature 'Suzanne') to a freelance publisher with the gift of the gab named Jeff Chase. The wrangles over the ownership of this troublesome triumvirate would bedevil Cohen throughout the next two decades. Indeed, a Hollywood film based solely on the narrative of the song 'Suzanne' was well into pre-production, with Cohen on board, before the producers discovered that the singer no longer owned the song. The project was immediately scrapped.

Around this time Cohen, ever the seeker of spiritual enlightenment, entered a brief period of devotion to the Californian cult of Scientology. It was a typically short-lived dalliance and one from which Cohen had some trouble escaping, after becoming predictably disillusioned with the dubious doctrines of the cult's figurehead L. Ron Hubbard. Nevertheless, it was at a Scientology convention he was attending at New York's Plaza hotel in 1968 that Cohen met the next in his parade of female accomplices.

Some sixteen years his junior, Suzanne Elrod strode into Cohen's life as she stepped from the same Plaza elevator he was about to enter. It was love at first sight. Floridan Suzanne (the name itself played no small part in captivating Cohen) was a smouldering brunette, the opposite to Marianne Ihlen's Nordic cool. Cohen wasted no time in introducing himself, and the self-assured 19-year-old showed no signs of aversion to the 35-year-old roué's advances. Within days Suzanne had quit her gold-digging affair with a rich New York business-man and had taken up residence in Cohen's Chelsea bolt hole. They did things that way in those days. Or at least Cohen certainly did.

Cohen chose Nashville as the place to record his second album, and rented a house with 12,000 acres of forested land in Franklin, south of the city, for the purpose from Everly Brothers songwriter Boudleaux Bryant. Naturally Suzanne went along. Tennessee would be Cohen's home for the next two years.

He had been drawn to Nashville for a number of reasons, not least of which was his abiding interest in country music, the genre that had so influenced The Buckskin Boys. Indeed Cohen has often remarked that he sees himself simply as a country singer. Nashville in 1968 was also a town in transition. Although still enshrined in ultra-conservative, God-fearing Southern mores, the town's deep-rooted traditionalism was undergoing a makeover, principally thanks to Bob Dylan.

Dylan had recorded part of *Blonde On Blonde* and both its successors at CBS's Nashville studios, employing the dextrous playing of the finest local musicians. This fairly revolutionary act had opened the gates of the citadel to the long-haired hordes, with everyone from Glen Campbell to Buffy Sainte-Marie recording there. Pretty soon country-rock, as personified by The Byrds, Gram Parsons and later even The Rolling Stones, would become the popular, rootsy alternative to outré psychedelia.

Enjoying the Hydra-like refuge of his Tennessee farm, coupled with the close proximity of a cosmopolitan centre, Cohen and Suzanne settled into a familiar pattern: he with his solitary writing, she with her pottery and needlework, the tranquility only interrupted by one or other of Cohen's fads. These included guns (Cohen owned several and liked to practice target-shooting deep in the woods) and horse-riding, as well as attempting various macrobiotic diets.

The album, eventually to be titled *Songs From A Room*, was produced by Bob Johnston, who had recently overseen Dylan's *Blonde On Blonde* masterpiece, as well as Johnny Cash's hit crossover album, *Fulsom Prison*. Johnston helped ease Cohen into the recording process, allowing him multiple takes and time to experiment with arrangements, while surrounding the singer with the most sympathetic players from Nashville's session regiments.

Between late 1968 and early 1969 Cohen busied himself with laying down the tracks for the album and befriending Nashville's musical aristocracy – striking up a firm friendship with, amongst others, singer-songwriter Kris Kristofferson.

If *Songs From A Room*, released in the spring of 1969 with pictures of Marianne in Cohen's Hydra home on the cover, was a far happier recording experience for Cohen than its predecessor, the results proved equally melancholy in tone, featuring such landmark compositions as 'Bird On A Wire' (perhaps Cohen's best known work after 'Suzanne') and 'The Old Revolution'. Reaching Number 2 in the British chart and 63 in the USA, the album built on the platform his debut had created and finally repaid John Hammond's faith in Cohen's commercial appeal. In Europe, particularly France and Spain, Cohen's star rose even above that of Dylan.

Italian film-maker Franco Zefferelli wanted Cohen to score the music for and star in a film about Saint Francis Of Assisi, but after a week-long hedonistic junket in Rome (where, coincidentally, he bumped into Nico, who once again refused his advances) Cohen lost interest and the part went to Donovan instead.

Later in the year, however, Cohen finally made his way onto the credits of a film when Robert Altman used three songs from his debut album on the soundtrack to the Julie Christie vehicle, *McCabe & Mrs Miller* – a failure at the box office on its release, the film is now revered as something of a cult classic.

In the summer of 1969 Cohen took a vacation from his Tennessee backwood and jetted out to the west coast. While in Los Angeles he attended the wedding of an old friend from Hydra, Steve Sanfield. Sanfield had been a dealer in antiques and drugs and had a taste for esoteric Eastern philosophies. After quitting Hydra in the mid-1960s he had found his way to California, where he had come under the influence of Zen Buddhism via a Japanese mission then situated in a small house in the unlikely location of a South Central Los Angeles suburb. Cohen had stayed in contact with Sanfield during his New York residency and was intrigued by his friend's new-found sense of calm, which he put down to the ascetic Rinzai brand of Buddhism practised at the mission.

Sanfield's wedding ceremony had been a Buddhist affair overseen by the mission leader, a 75-year-old Zen Master named Joshu Sasaki Roshi. As well as the expected rituals of cleansing meditation and hushed chanting, the ceremony involved the copious quaffing of sake and much laughter. Unsurprisingly, Cohen was hooked. Spiritual ceremony, hedonism and the ritual of love taken together constituted an irresistible cocktail of attractions.

At the beginning of 1969 Jack McClelland published Cohen's *Selected Poems, 1956–1968*. It was a timely reprising of the singer's other career and helped reinvigorate his reputation as a songwriter. It may have been Dylan who was often referred to as a poet, but Cohen was the genuine, published article.

The collection was well received and in April Cohen was awarded Canada's prestigious Governor-General's Award For Poetry – which he turned down. He wasn't ready for the Academy, and besides it was the sort of contentious action his mentor Irving Layton was prone to do, although Layton had actually accepted a previous Governor-General's Award.

In the summer of 1970 Cohen capitalised on his rippling fame by undertaking his first major concert tour. His appeal in North America was still limited to the coastal conurbations. So, rather than plot a geographically complicated campaign through Middle America, he chose to concentrate on Europe, where his fan base was both more ardent and more evenly spread.

Beginning in Germany and taking in Scandinavia, France and England, Cohen and his band, which included Charlie Daniels – later to have a hit with 'The Devil Went Down To Georgia' – and Bob Johnston, and named The Army after surviving a night of bottle-throwing communist students in the south of France, wowed primed and expectant audiences with loose, semi-improvised versions of songs from Cohen's two albums, interspersed with poetry recitations and sardonic monologues, often at the singer's own expense.

In Hamburg he entertained the crowd with some less-than-subtle Sieg Heil salutes. In Copenhagen he led the crowd out into the streets at the concert's close. In Aix-en-Provence he took to the stage dressed in cowboy garb on the back of a white horse. It was all a long way from the reverent, lounge-suited image of the latter-day Cohen, and very much in the improvisatory spirit of the times. He was beginning to relish the proximity to his audience after years of self-imposed exile from it.

In England he played to a rapt 10,000-strong Royal Albert Hall audience and then, during the August Bank Holiday weekend, motored down to the south coast to appear at The Isle Of Wight Festival. Despite not taking the stage until an enthusiasm-sapping 4am and having to follow Jimi Hendrix's famous pyrotechnic set, the reception was warm. For many, including Nashville comrade Kris Kristofferson who was deeply moved, he stole the show.

To facilitate his new-found enchantment with the live arena, Cohen needed capable and trustworthy management. He had become frustrated with Mary Martin's inability to sort out the farrago over the song rights still held by Jeff Chase, and so had ended their Stranger Music partnership in early 1970. In her place he appointed Marty Machat as overseer of his financial affairs. Machat, a New York lawyer and theatrical producer, was Bob Johnston's legal adviser and knew the labyrinths of entertainment law better than most. He would stay at Cohen's right hand until his death in the mid-1980s.

Cohen's reputation continued to grow through the early

1970s as his novel and poetry were translated into several European languages, and Canadian colleges were tripping over themselves to present him with awards.

On the crest of a wave, he was soon back in Nashville preparing to record his third album. It was at this point that Cohen began to have serious doubts about his abilities as a musician. Much had been made of his croaky, baritone singing voice (in yet another parallel with Dylan, Cohen was ridiculed as much for the singularity of his singing style as for the complexity of his lyrics) and, on re-entering the recording studio, he started to take the criticisms to heart.

To add to this dilemma, his relationship with Suzanne was entering a trough. She resented the amount of time he was spending away from her. A familiar pattern began to emerge. The more she pressed Cohen, the more claustrophobic he felt, forcing him to recoil even further from her. He took to roaming his vast Tennessee acreage or in locked-door solitude, poring over the I-Ching and other Zen-related texts.

With his confidence low, recording of his third album, revealingly titled *Songs Of Love & Hate*, ground on throughout March 1971. Once again Bob Johnston was at the helm, and once again a pall of melancholy seemed to have commandeered Cohen's vocal booth. The tone of the songs was relentless. The suicidal 'Avalanche' (curiously released as a single in Europe) morphed sombrely into the dreary 'Joan Of Arc' (another paean of unrequited love to Nico, written back in Cohen's Chelsea Hotel days), and the listless 'Last Year's Man' into the maudlin 'Dress Rehearsal Rag', onto which the poignant children's voices were overdubbed during a post-Nashville session in London.

For the first time critics began to apply their sharpest scalpels to Cohen's songs. The reaction to the album's midsummer release was muted at best, excoriating at worst. Cohen was perceived to be wallowing in his own pain and, after two albums' worth of such depressive fare it was generally felt that the visionary poet was in a creative rut. Nothing he said at the time seemed to contradict these opinions. To one journalist he drolly described the album as the 'same old droning work, an inch or two forward.'

Under such clouds of melancholy, Cohen was easily enticed back onto the road. It was a kind of escapism but also – his stage nerves for the most part now vanquished – the opportunity to commune with his audience and regain some creative confidence.

The 1972 tour was a much more extensive affair than its predecessor, taking in 21 concerts in 20 cities throughout March and April. First time visits to Ireland, Scotland, the Netherlands, Belgium and Austria, as well as triumphant returns to West Germany and England, culminated in a series of concerts in Israel which Cohen mischievously painted as a kind of homecoming.

Bob Johnston played keyboards, but otherwise this was an entirely new Army, composed of Los Angeles session eminences. Also recruited for the tour were two female backing vocalists ostensibly employed to assuage Cohen's increasing lack of confidence in his own vault-like baritone. One of these was Seattle-born, California-raised Jennifer Warnes, destined to duet with Joe Cocker and Bill Medley in the 1980s. A talented musician in her own right, her career would intertwine with Cohen's for the next two decades. During the tour the two became close (though, miraculously, not lovers) and wrote a song together, 'Song Of Bernadette' which appeared on Warnes's hit 1987 album, *Famous Blue Raincoat*, comprised solely of Cohen compositions.

Drugs played a more significant part in proceedings than in 1970. Cohen performed part of his Jerusalem concert on acid, which led to him seeing 'Biblical visions' and bursting into uncontrollable floods of tears onstage.

Such was his disdain for his more recent material that he played only three or four songs a night from *Songs Of Love & Hate*, drawing instead on the first two albums and a clutch of folk chestnuts and standards (including Cole Porter's 'As Time Goes By') to bulk out the 17-song set.

Despite – or perhaps because of – the tour being something of a triumph, its end signalled a return to the state of depression that had afflicted him during the making of the third album. Being back with Suzanne didn't help. She had become pregnant at the turn of the year, and the prospect of parenthood seemed to have little effect on their torrid relationship other than to increase Cohen's drug use (cocaine had now entered the fray) and to drive him deeper into his reading of Eastern philosophy.

In September 1972 Suzanne gave birth to a son, Adam, and Cohen settled into his new Montreal home with lover and child for an all too short-lived period of domestic tranquility. He was not at the birth. At the time he was in London discussing the setting up of a publishing house, to be called Spice-Box Books. When the call came to say that Adam had been born, Cohen received the news with little enthusiasm. Earlier that day he'd heard that his childhood friend Robert Hershorn had died in mysterious circumstances in Hong Kong. Cohen returned to Montreal to wet his baby's head and bury an old friend. As ever, his moment of joy was shaded with sadness.

It wasn't long before a familiar *déjà vu* began to pervade the Montreal home, with Cohen at once the doting father and increasingly hemmed-in lover. It was Hydra and Marianne all over again.

His escape this time came by way of Zen Buddhism and the welcoming disciplines of Joshu Sasaki Roshi, who was now installed in a monastery high up on Mount Baldy in the St. Gabriel ranges north of Los Angeles. Cohen stayed for just over three weeks, close-cropping his hair, observing the 3am wake-up calls, trudging through the Mount Baldy snow in sandals and practising meditation.

Three weeks was enough for him. It was principally the numbing cold that got to him, and soon he was heading south for the comforting warmth of the Mexican sun. There Suzanne joined him for a brief holiday before the two returned to Montreal.

Once home, Cohen oversaw the publication of his latest collection of poetry, initially titled *Songs Of Disobedience* but published as *The Energy Of Slaves*. A certain creative entropy was reflected in the fact that most of the poems dated back to the mid-to-late-1960s – one had even been written as long ago as 1961 and his Havana sojourn. Unsurprisingly, the mood of the book, like the record that preceded it, was negative. Cohen has called it 'an inferno of self and self-hatred', and it is easily the most dour and alienating piece of work he has presented to the public in any form. It did nothing to change the general perception of Cohen as the poet laureate of gloom.

In April 1973, *Live Songs* was released to fill the void left by Cohen's first substantial blocked period as a writer. Drawn from recordings made during the two European tours, *Live Songs* stands as an interesting document of those early forays but, once again, the music – stripped of audience euphoria or the dark humour that was a crucial part of the onstage presentation – seemed mired in despondency. The sleeve notes were written by the manic depressive English poet Daphne Richardson, who had become a regular correspondent of Cohen's during the early 1970s. True to the spirit of Cohen's moribund reputation, Richardson took her own life before the album was even released, by jumping off the roof of the BBC's Bush House building in central London.

Rumours abounded that Cohen was about to retire. He was said to be disillusioned with the music industry and seemed bereft of new ideas. It wasn't true, though in scotching the rumours in typically laconic style he more than alluded to his overriding sense of futility: 'What is there to quit?' he asked a reporter from the Toronto Star. He may not have been joking.

In the summer of 1973 a Broadway play opened based on Cohen's songs. Titled *Sisters Of Mercy* after the hymnal song from the first album, the play was critically panned (Cohen himself hated it) and closed quickly. It was another nail in the coffin of a once healthy career. Cohen, with Suzanne and Adam in tow, returned to the relative peace of Hydra, where he could lick his wounds and begin to scan the horizon for more efficacious enterprises.

One such diversion was the Yom Kippur war between Israel and Egypt which flared up in October. Cohen had followed the political dogfighting between the two religiously attrition-al nations and saw becoming personally involved in the war as an opportunity to cast off the relatively petty yoke of the music industry. It would also relieve the pressure on his still volatile relationship with Suzanne.

In late September he flew from Athens to Tel Aviv with the object of joining the Israeli army. This proved difficult. The war was confined to the Israeli-Egyptian border and life in sunny Tel Aviv went on mostly unaffected, save for blackout curtains and the odd radio report from the front line.

Cohen stayed with relatives of a fellow passenger he had met on the flight over, wishing to blend into normal society. He even made a pact with himself to refrain from libidinous activities while in the Holy Land. This lasted for all of a week before he became preoccupied with the usual litany of sexual conquests. One female reporter who tracked him down to Tel Aviv's Gad Hotel, where he later stayed, was even made to remove her top before he would agree to an interview.

Despite the diversions, his lack of Hebrew and a belief that the Arab side actually had a genuine grievance against the Jews (who had seized land from Egypt during the previous decade's Six Day War), Cohen was still determined to join up. Eventually he did so via the invitation of local folk singer Solomo Semach, who placed Cohen with an Air Force entertainment troupe and furnished him with a guitar.

Cohen was helicoptered to the front line, where he performed at rocket-launching sites and for bivouacked tank squadrons. Deep in the Sinai desert he was introduced to and sipped Cognac with the Israeli General Sharon, himself a Cohen fan and, much later, the scourge of the PLO. Once or twice the concert party even came under fire.

The sight of captured, wounded Egyptian troops pricked his conscience and, although he observed a certain nobility in the soldiers and airmen with whom he mingled, Cohen soon grew disillusioned with the war and, after a short break in Jerusalem, left Israel for Greece.

The thought of plunging back into domestic strife, however, perplexed him and instead of going home he took a plane to Ethiopia where, in his Asmara hotel room, he considered his future and wrote some songs, including the sardonic 'Field Commander Cohen' and the final version of 'Chelsea Hotel #2'.

Eventually he returned to Greece and Suzanne. Things in the familial home were still uneasy, and throughout 1974 Cohen blotted them out by concentrating on his Zen meditations, periods of fasting and some sustained attempts to write his memoirs. He was 41.

But he had not abandoned songwriting. Some of the material he had begun in Ethiopia was coaxed into completion in his Hydra music room and his appetite for album-making was slowly rekindled.

New Skin For The Old Ceremony was released at the height of summer 1974 and had the effect of reminding the world of Cohen's potency as a writer of emotive lyrics and opulent melodies. There was an undertow of dark humour that had been missing on *Songs Of Love & Hate* and the terse 11-song album did much to challenge his still pervading image as the lachrymose miser of joy.

'Chelsea Hotel' finally saw the light of day and the relatively bouncy 'Lover, Lover, Lover' (written in the Israeli desert) proved he could master a certain up-tempo brio; while 'Who By Fire' showed his evocative way with a Biblical epithet had not abandoned him.

Produced in New York by John Lissauer with an economical but always alluring sonic palette featuring delicate string arrangements and muted brass, the album was well received by critics on both sides of the Atlantic. It was generally regarded as a return to form, and in some cases even as a minor classic. With the release of 'Lover Lover Lover' as a 7-inch single, Cohen also had his first hit since 'Avalanche' similarly tickled the lower reaches of various Scandinavian and Benelux charts in 1971. Only the album's artwork caused any ripples of disquiet. Depicting two naked, flying angels apparently enjoying sexual congress (the image was a woodcut purloined from an arcane 16th-century tome), it was with-drawn from sale in America and a standard portrait of Cohen put in its place. *New Skin For The Old Ceremony* failed to trouble the American charts, but reached Number 24 in Britain, while sales were still healthy in Canada and mainland Europe.

So happy was Cohen with his renaissance as a recording artist (and with Lissauer's élan as an orchestrator) that he quickly returned to CBS's New York studios at the end of 1974 to record a follow-up. Six songs were committed to tape, including an early version of 'Came So Far For Beauty'. The song would eventually appear on 1979's *Recent Songs*, and the putative album, possibly to be titled *Songs For Rebecca*, was soon shelved, where it remains, to the chagrin of the bootleggers, to this day.

In the autumn of 1974 Suzanne gave birth to a daughter, Lorca, and, perhaps not coincidentally, Cohen felt the lure of the boards once more and set out on his third European tour.

Spread over nearly two months and taking in thirty-three concerts, Cohen's European stock showed no signs of falling. A first visit to Spain acknowledged his vast popularity there (his new songs were always immediately translated into a Spanish language songbook) and Cohen returned the compli-ment by dedicating his Barcelona show to the memory of Federico Garcia Lorca.

At the end of the year he even essayed a short North American tour, his first of any magnitude, selling out venues in New York and Los Angeles and ending up in Montreal. His show at the tiny Theatre du Monde was his first hometown appearance in 15 years and, although exhausted from his gru-elling tour schedule, he gave a moving performance, including a version of 'Bird On The Wire' sung in French.

By the spring of 1975 Cohen was back on Hydra undergoing another in his series of self-dissections, and bemoaning the fact that success had brought him no nearer to a sense of fulfilment or happiness. Even his continual pursuit of women seemed little more than a futile gesture to recapture the flame of youth, a lost time of freedom from expectation. Not that such concerns ever actually interrupted his philandering. A string of liaisons ensued throughout 1974, all of them nominally behind Suzanne's back. One encounter even led to a bout of gonorrhoea, which an Athens doctor had to attend to with penicillin shots. Cohen's womanising went on undeterred.

Tourism rather than touring occupied much of 1975. Cohen took a trip with the Zen Master Roshi to the monasteries of Japan and then made a short reading tour of Italy, where much of his work had been recently translated. He stayed on in Florence and Rome, enraptured by the elegant young women and mulling over the fanciful notion of joining the Italian Communist Party.

At the end of the year he was back in Montreal. He had not become a communist, but he was again writing songs. Before he could develop these, Columbia insisted on his overseeing the release of a Greatest Hits project (after the release of just four studio albums) designed to capitalise on a new generation of young fans for whom Cohen was more a 1970s musical *éminence grise* than a 1960s folk tyro. Cohen was happy to oblige – penning laconic liner notes to each song and once again hitting the road to promote the record.

The 1976 tour was the longest yet – lasting nearly three months with fifty-six marathon shows, often containing more than thirty songs on a given night. The tone of these concerts was less portentous than had previously been the case, a fact evinced by Cohen's inclusion of the uncharacteristically insouciant standard 'You Are My Sunshine', a version that owed much to Ray Charles's reading. Otherwise, the programme drew on the core of his four studio albums and even made room for some unrecorded material from the mid-1960s, namely 'Everybody's Child' and 'The Store Room'. There was also a surprisingly propulsive new song (it had a 'definite rock quality' according to one London critic) called 'Do I have To Dance All Night?' which proved something of a show-stopper. Alas, it has never been recorded.

After the tour Cohen returned to Hydra and the embraces of Zen. Later in the year he spent time reacquainting himself with elements of the Jewish faith during extended sojourns in Montreal. Again, the spiritual questing acted as an interiorising counterpoint to all the public exposure that had preceded it. Escape from the ruins of his moribund relationship with Suzanne was a bonus of these solitary studies.

This time the tour concentrated on Europe – still by far the most lucrative and sympathetic marketplace for Cohen's wares – and the critical reaction was universally positive, if only in celebration of Cohen's palpable lack of glumness.

Of all Cohen's musical accomplices over the years, none has been more unlikely than Phil Spector. Spector was the maverick production svengali behind 1960s hit acts The Ronettes, The Crystals and Ike & Tina Turner, whose thunderous 'River Deep, Mountain High' single defined his trademark Wall Of Sound. Latterly Spector had been applying his multi-textured signature to albums by John Lennon, Harry Nilsson and Dion, and was again in favour with the Los Angeles cognoscenti after a period of myth-sustaining silence.

Spector's lawyer was Marty Machat, who was still looking after Cohen's affairs, and through him the two were introduced with the idea of recording together. In fact they had met briefly after Cohen's run of shows at The Troubadour Theater, Los Angeles in the autumn of 1974. Mutual intrigue was the result.

It was not a marriage made in heaven. On the face of it, Cohen's introspective songwriting and intimate lyrics were diametrically opposed to Spector's euphoric *sturm und drang*. Remarkably, they hit it off during a tentative 1977 Los Angeles writing session (despite Spector's penchant for sub-zero air conditioning) and agreed to work on an album together.

Cohen saw Spector as a vehicle for broadening the appeal of his songwriting. Spector, in turn, would only gain gravitas by applying his sonic panoply to the era's premier songwriting poet. This was all very well in theory, but in practice their antithetical approaches to music-making made for some turbulent sessions at Los Angeles's Gold Star studios, where they were holed up for much of the summer of 1977.

Spector's habit of explaining his requirements to musicians while brandishing a wine bottle in one hand and a cocked shotgun in the other made for an unnerving atmosphere. Several musicians walked out of the sessions and Cohen himself was included in proceedings only after Spector had spent many hours meticulously laying down the 30 to 40 different instruments that were to provide the backing tracks. When Cohen was eventually summoned to the microphone he was allowed just a single take to get his vocals down – something about which he consistently complained in subsequent years.

Such was the curiosity of the local music scene that visitors were common to the studio, if they could negotiate Spector's retinue of bodyguards. Most describe the army of musicians as tense and agitated, with Spector dashing amongst them with wild, tyrannical zeal while Cohen sat cross-legged in a corner, meditating.

On one occasion Bob Dylan turned up after attending an Allen Ginsberg reading at the Troubadour on Sunset Boulevard. With Ginsberg in tow, Dylan (along with the requisite cast of thousands) was roped in to sing backing vocals on the fulminating choruses of the splendidly provocative 'Don't Go Home With Your Hard-On'.

The resulting *Death Of A Ladies' Man* was like nothing Cohen had put his name to before. The cavernous arrangements dominated the vocals. Cohen's strangled larynx is occasionally reduced to a distant tremor amid the salvos of brass, cascades of strings and phalanxes of choir-like backing vocals, but the result is an often mesmerising juggernaut of a record that teeters continually between the kitsch and the sublime.

Despite the Cohen/Spector credits, much of the material on *Death Of A Ladies' Man* was not new. 'True Love Leaves No Traces' was based on the 1958 poem 'As The Mist Leaves No Scar', 'Iodine' was a rewrite of a song called 'Guerrero', which Cohen had been performing live on and off since 1975, while the lyrics to 'Fingerprints' were lifted wholesale from the 1966 poem 'Give Me Back My Fingerprints'.

On its release in November 1977 the album, not unsurprisingly, divided critical opinion, with the majority ignorantly coming out against. The incongruity of pop symphonia and visceral, sexually explicit lyrics seemed to baffle most. Only the English critics found anything redeeming in the incongruous mismatch – The Doyen Of Doom Meets Teen Tycoon, as one memorable headline read.

Cohen himself was rather smitten with the record. Though

still resentful about being barred from polishing his vocal performances, he nonetheless pronounced the much-maligned orchestrations 'brilliant', but he soon sought to distance himself from the project when the critical invective started rolling in.

Many of the lyrics on *Death Of A Ladies' Man* were penned during several frenetic writing bursts that Cohen threw himself into during the latter half of 1976. As well as these lyrics, a slew of poetry and prose poured onto the page from his trusty Olivetti with a profligacy unmatched since his early-1960s salad days. The resulting verse was eventually published as the (subtly spelt) *Death Of A Lady's Man* collection.

If Cohen had gained a reputation for being an acuitous and disciplined self-editor, then this latest project took his revisionism to new heights. Cohen had informed McClelland & Stewart that the manuscript would be complete by the autumn of 1976, but he was finally satisfied that the work was complete only after half a dozen rewrites, and the book eventually appeared on bookshop shelves a full two years later, in September 1978.

As was becoming the norm, the reviews were mixed. Jack McClelland secretly wondered if the original 1976 manuscript wouldn't have been better. But Cohen's worry over the collection had been compounded by the recording work with Phil Spector and by frequent visits to Montreal to visit his now elderly and ailing mother.

More significantly for Cohen the artist, the book's peculiar lack of acknowledgement (not a single review appeared in America) signalled his drift from the literary world. After 10 years as an itinerant troubadour, he was now perceived first and foremost as a singer-songwriter with a literary background, in marked contrast to the 1967 perceptions of Columbia's A&R department who (with the noble exception of John Hammond) prophesied that the poet would never make a career in music.

At the end of 1977 Cohen moved back to Montreal to be with his dying mother. It was also an opportunity to enjoy his rapidly growing children and to patch things up, yet again, with Suzanne.

Masha Cohen died of leukaemia the following February. After overseeing the funeral and the division of the estate, Cohen moved his fragile family out to Los Angeles where he was keen to start work on a new album. The location also meant easy access to the monastery at Mount Baldy and its twin Zen centre located in the city's southern suburbs.

Shortly after the relocation, Cohen's decade-long affair with Suzanne finally came to a close. After all the in-fighting, they had finally drifted too far apart to meaningfully sustain the relationship and in April Suzanne and the children left to start a new life in Paris.

Cohen was initially perturbed by their leaving, especially as it came so soon after the mourning of his mother, but, unsurprisingly, he soon got over it. Within weeks he was relishing his freedom, yet he saw it, remarkably, not as a green light for his usual womanising but as a clean slate for his working life. He began to work out, to swim and to make daily visits to the Zen centre for meditation. He also began to re-apply himself to typewriter and guitar.

Cohen had been recommended the production talents of Henry Lewry by his old friend and now Hollywood Hills neighbour, Joni Mitchell. Cohen played Lewry his latest compositions on the terrace of the singer's impressive new Woodrow Wilson Avenue house and the producer was duly impressed. So much so, in fact, that he suggested an immediate recording date using Mitchell's backing group, Passenger. Among their number were future Cohen producer Roscoe Beck on bass and long-term live cohort Steve Meador on drums. They gathered at United Western Studios that evening and swiftly cut the track 'The Smokey Life', initially earmarked as the title track of the album that would emerge as *Recent Songs*.

Lewry then arranged a more orthodox session plan at A&M studios and drafted in other musicians, including old bastions Jennifer Warnes on backing vocals and John Lissauer on keyboards. He also invited oud player John Bilezikjian to contribute the exotic tones of his middle-eastern instrument to the mix. Cohen himself enlisted the services of a violin player named Raffi Hakopian, whom he heard playing in a Los Angeles bar (and whose soloing on the album's highlight, 'The Guests', is some of the most exquisite accompaniment on any Cohen record). The Band's bear-like keyboard genius Garth Hudson was among the guest players, put to work after paying a social visit to Cohen *in situ*.

Recent Songs returned Cohen to the pared-down arrangements of his early albums, and stood in stark contrast to the bellicose bravura of its Spector-produced predecessor. Songs such as 'The Gypsy's Wife', 'Came So Far For Beauty' and 'The Lost Canadian' were melancholy torch songs which nevertheless appeared brisk and conversational by comparison with the elegiac mien of his most famous works.

Cohen's deep, warm vocals were once again at the front of a mix that was also distinguished by its delicate interplay of mostly acoustic instruments. Jennifer Warnes's keening harmonies were interwoven with graceful adroitness, and everywhere the music seemed to ebb and flow with unforced ease. It was a genuine return to form, and one that was acknowledged by an approving press and sold-out concerts for the world tour that followed the album's September 1979 release. Oddly, it was Cohen's only real failure in Canada.

With a winter 1979 leg throughout Europe and a spring 1980 excursion to Australia (his first visit there), the tour represented Cohen's most concerted promotional activity to date. The dextrous band, once more mostly drawn from the Los Angeles recording ensemble, made for agreeably sophisticated concerts, with Warnes and harmony partner Sharon Robinson proving gossamer foils for Cohen's ever more dolorous vocalising.

The tour was filmed by Canadian documentary-maker Harry Rasky and the resulting CBC programme, *Song Of Leonard Cohen*, shows the subject looking tanned, trim and smiling a lot. He was clearly not missing Suzanne.

He was, however, missing his children, and the wrangle over custody rights meandered on into the mid-1980s by which time Adam and Lorca were old enough to make up their own minds about where they wanted to live. When Suzanne moved the family to the south of France in the early 1980s (the house, like the Paris abode before it, were purchased by Cohen) he followed, even staying for a time in a trailer at the perimeter of the grounds so as not to infringe the legal stipulations.

The year 1980 found Cohen spending more and more time in the company of Zen Master Roshi. Although his devotion to Zen Buddhism and its central tenets of ego-less one-ness with self, were precious to Cohen, he never declared himself a Zen Buddhist, preferring instead to refer to himself as a practitioner of Zen. He once flippantly remarked that what drew him to Roshi was his teacher's generosity with the monastery sake. For all that, Cohen's Jewish faith had never deserted him entirely, and he continued to celebrate rituals like Hanukkah and carried a copy of the Talmud in his luggage at all times.

In October 1980 a buoyant Cohen began yet another European tour, his sixth. Revisiting the countries that loved him best – France, Germany and England – Cohen and Passenger (minus Jennifer Warnes) once again played to full houses and gained the approbation of reviewers. His star was beaming again.

In contrast to the rollercoaster that was Cohen's 1960s and 1970s love life, the 1980s proved to be a period of relative stability with regards to matters of the heart. In 1982 he met Dominique Isserman, a Parisian fashion photographer who was holidaying on Hydra. Their affair lasted throughout the first half of the decade, and never descended into the fractious mind games that characterised Cohen's dealings with Suzanne. He was careful never to live with Dominique for any extended period. Instead the two got on with their separate lives, then spent time together on Hydra, in Paris or in Montreal whenever their schedules allowed. Although they eventually drifted apart romantically, they remain firm friends – Dominique shot the videos for Cohen's late-1980s singles. Approaching 50, Cohen had learned his lesson and was beginning to enjoy a less frenetic maturity.

Around the same time that he met Dominique, Cohen was working on the libretto for an opera he had undertaken in tandem with composer Lewis Furey (who had played viola on *New Skin For The Old Ceremony*). Entitled *Night Magic*, (after a line in Van Morrison's 'Moondance' and a Montreal nightclub called Nuit Magique), the story revolved around the fantasies of a down-at-heel Montreal folk singer. Cohen described it as a cross between Brecht and Disney. The finished opera was well received and a film version made it as far as the 1985 Cannes Film Festival. Cohen and Furey even picked up a gong for Best Music Score at that year's Canadian Juno awards ceremony.

Flushed a little with the success of this enterprise, Cohen had an idea for a film to be called *I Am A Hotel* – a partly autobiographical piece based on Cohen's twenty-plus years' experience of being a guest at some of the world's most celebrated hostelries. Although promises of funding came and went, and the network for which it was originally intended – Canadian pay-TV company C-Channel – went bust, the short, surrealistic, dialogue-free movie was eventually finished under the auspices of a Toronto broadcast company, City-TV.

Utilising five songs from Cohen's 16-year back catalogue, the film hazily depicts a human tide of figures moving in and out of mocked-up hotel rooms, with only the music hinting at the psychological narratives unfolding behind the actors' mask-like faces.

Cohen demanded a re-shoot and many edits were undertaken (this was a Leonard Cohen project, after all) by director Don Allen. It was worth the effort. *I Am A Hotel* garnered many plaudits, winning the Golden Rose at the 24th Montreux Television Festival and re-alerting the world to the evocativeness of Cohen's songs and his willingness to adapt to the art forms of the age.

To counterbalance the zeitgeist-surfing, Cohen applied himself to the writing of 50 psalms (to match his half-century in years), initially titled *The Shield* but, inevitably, altered on publication to *The Book Of Mercy*. The book's April release found several critics wondering how the flashing vitriol of *Death Of A Ladies' Man* could be so swiftly superseded by such mystical piety. Yet many warmed to the book's elegant Old Testament language and spiritual tone. In July 1985 the book won a prize from the Canadian Author's Association.

Music was soon interesting Cohen again, perhaps partly as a result of his name being dropped by a host of young artists then being lauded by the European music press. With such vaunted acolytes as Nick Cave, Ian McCulloch of Echo & The Bunnymen and David McComb of hotly tipped Australians The Triffids all mentioning Cohen's influence in gushing, venerating tones, his popularity was rising again.

This was a doubly useful thing for Cohen: the reality of his film-making, upkeep of several houses and financial support for his children meant he was flat broke.

Enlisting the aid of John Lissauer and a host of backing musicians, Cohen cut *Various Positions* in New York at the tail end of 1984. He had been whittling away at songs throughout much of the year, and for the first time wrote much of the material on piano and a newly acquired synthe-sizer, rather than his habitual guitar. A countryish feel never-theless pervades the album's nine reverberant tracks, with the lyrics perched midway between evangelical sermonising and parochial-sounding yarns. Songs like 'The Law' and 'If It Be Your Will' (with Jennifer Warnes at her glorious best) draw on Jewish religious imagery, while 'The Captain' and 'The Night Comes On' are, by turns, jaunty and achingly autobio-graphical, with a dry, self-deprecating sense of humour dotted here and there amid the elegiac poetic imagery.

Again Europe proved receptive, with Cohen touring through much of the summer of 1985. In the era of Madonna's *Like A Virgin*, Bruce Springsteen's *Born In The USA* and the Live Aid phenomenon, CBS in New York didn't see a place for Cohen and, scandalously, failed to release the record at all in America. Despite such corporate reluctance, in May he had played his first New York concert in 10 years to a packed

Carnegie Hall. Cohen bemoaned the lack of faith from his American label managers, but once again revelled in the untrammelled affection of German, French, Scandinavian and English audiences and seemed resigned to his Europhone fate.

During the early 1980s Cohen had maintained his platonic relationship with Jennifer Warnes, comforting her when her boyfriend was killed in an automobile accident and providing encouragement for her singing career. In 1985 Warnes hit on the idea of an album of Cohen originals. Cohen himself was less than keen on the idea, a scepticism shared by the majority of record companies whom Warnes approached.

Eventually the independent Cypress Records became interested and Warnes set about recording, with old Cohen sideman Roscoe Beck in the production chair. Although initially cool about the project, Cohen slowly became involved, making regular unbidden appearances at Los Angeles's The Complex, where the sessions took place, duetting on 'Joan Of Arc' and even supplying a new song he'd written after a 1984 exchange with Warnes on the subject of the then rampant AIDS virus. The song, 'Ain't No Cure For Love', was to be one of the highlights of the album Warnes christened *Famous Blue Raincoat* (she had rejected Cohen's title suggestion, *Jenny Sings Lenny*) that was an unexpected hit on its eventual release in 1987.

In between times Cohen busied himself with songwriting and the odd maverick diversion, like taking a cameo role in the hit television series *Miami Vice* (he played the head of Interpol, but his acting skills were meagre and his part still languishes on the cutting room floor) and singing on a compilation album dedicated to the work of his hero Federico Garcia Lorca. Cohen's contribution was the song 'Take This Waltz', itself based on a Lorca verse, which would appear on his next album, *I'm Your Man*.

I'm Your Man was as laborious to write as it was easy on the ear. Cohen had toiled and anguished over some of the songs for more than two years, and was still revising lines during the final mix sessions. Many of the lyrics were inspired by renewed reading of various Hasidic texts and by the self-help book *The Positive Value Of Depression*. Cohen's droll sense of humour was once again in evidence.

Utilising much of the team that had worked on Warnes's LP – with Roscoe Beck in the production chair – *I'm Your Man* was imbued with an entirely new Leonard Cohen sound, one that was emblematic of a new-found confidence and a willingness to join in with the musical world of the 1980s. CBS even deigned to release the record in America.

The sonic signature of *I'm Your Man* came as a shock to many Cohen fans. This was a thoroughly modern, highly produced and glossy-sounding record. Phalanxes of shimmering keyboards and pulsating sequencers replaced the Spanish guitar and Jew's harp of yore, while Cohen's sonorous ocean-floor intoning was bathed in spectral echo and caressed by choir-like backing vocals.

The songs were the genuine article, all the same. From the delirious meta-doo-wop of 'Ain't No Cure For Love' through the Brechtian eurodisco of 'First We Take Manhattan', lilting 'I Can't Forget' and whimsical title track, Cohen commands the plangent tableau with a laconic hipster's aplomb. Oud player John Bilezikjian and violinist Raffi Hakopian both turn in inspired performances and the harmonious sonic tapestry throughout confers on *I'm Your Man* the honour of being Cohen's most fully-realised album.

The 1988 I'm Your Man tour was an appropriately marathon odyssey in support of what was a career-revitalising

LP. During it Cohen would sing part of the set in crooner's style – abandoning for the first time his trademark Gibson acoustic and clutching the microphone like a sacrament, his eyes shut tight with the exertion. One highlight of the 1988 sets was the LP's closing track 'Tower Of Song', perhaps Cohen's best-loved post-'60s song. The plaintive paean to the vocalists that have gone before contains the ironic line, 'I was born with the gift of a golden voice', which, when delivered with Cohen's most speaker-worrying *basso profundo*, would elicit spontaneous cheers of approval from his adoring audiences on a nightly basis.

Sixty cities in three and a half months represented a mighty undertaking for a 53-year-old – especially as the shows would regularly run to two and a half hours with encores, but Cohen was fit and relatively happy and felt re-nourished by the warmth of his audience's response.

The Cohen publicity machine clicked into overdrive. Much of the tour was recorded for both sound and vision. Cohen popped up on a variety of television shows – mostly on European stations but also, memorably, on the Austin City Limits show – his first full concert performance to be shown on American television and as good a promotional device as any amount of touring in what was still the least receptive market in which his records were sold. In another remarkable broadcast (on saxophonist David Sanborn's late-night New York show) jazz great Sonny Rollins joined the stripped-down band for a euphonious reading of 'Who By Fire'.

Cohen was now used to such excellence. His band, with John Bilezikjian to the fore, Perla Batalla and Julie Christensen (Cohen's 'angels') on sultry backing vocals and Steve Meador once more on drums, was a well-oiled octet, as adept at reproducing the mechanised sound of *I'm Your Man* as it was adding subtle shading to the frontman's nominally solo renditions of 'Suzanne' or 'Avalanche'.

At the itinerary's end an exhausted Cohen returned to Los Angeles and the usual post-tour ennui. He was now a major international star, eclipsing even the celebrity of his late-1960s heyday. But he was still morose. Zen meditation was soon complimented by doses of the depressive's panacea *du jour*, Prozac. Women still preoccupied him but, with Dominique now departed, his old ways became curbed to some extent. Even a Lothario of Cohen's insatiable stamina has to draw in his horns at the age of 54, or so it seems.

At a party in Paris in 1986 Cohen had been introduced to the Hollywood actress Rebecca De Mornay. They had stayed in touch during the *I'm Your Man* period and in 1990 they began a brief romance, despite an age difference of some 18 years. Rebecca was an insightful and well-read thirtysomething and not of the usual vacuous Hollywood stock. She was influential in the creation of Cohen's next body of songs (she is even credited with producing one track) and their involvement led to Cohen appearing in the world's gossip pages, something which amused him greatly.

In 1990 a Hollywood film entitled *Bird On The Wire* starring Goldie Hawn was released, the same year Cohen songs were covered by artists as disparate as Concrete Blonde and The Neville Brothers.

His fame was passed on to a new generation of aficionados when the tribute album *I'm Your Fan* was released in 1991. Originally the frivolous notion of Pixies frontman Black Francis (later known as Frank Black) in idle conversation with French rock writer Christian Fevret, *I'm Your Fan* featured some of Cohen's most accessible material given the alternative rock treatment by REM, Nick Cave, James,

Pixies and John Cale. It was a considerable success and cemented to the pedestal reserved for revered 1960s survivors – one he would share with Dylan – himself enjoying a critical renaissance on the back of his *Oh Mercy!* album.

Riding this crest of popularity, Cohen began to consider another album. Living in Los Angeles at the time of the 1992 riots was the inspiration for some of the songs that ended up on what is still Cohen's most recent studio album, *The Future*. The riots followed an incident in which white members of the L.A.P.D. were videotaped in the process of beating up a solitary black male named Rodney King. Los Angeles was a tense and, for a while, dangerous place for a white man in a well-tailored suit (Cohen's preferred dress throughout the 1980s and early 1990s) to be. He was by now living in a house close to the South Central epicentre of black indignation and was able to witness the anger, looting and burning at first hand.

Many of the songs on *The Future* (original title: *Busted*) were several years old, but recent events found their way into rewritten verses of songs like 'Democracy', 'Closing Time' and the title track (original title: 'If You Could See What Was Coming Next'). Cohen laboured long and hard over the songs – a single song lyric would have 50 or 60 rewrites before he stepped near a microphone. Rebecca De Mornay was used as a sounding board for much of Cohen's early 1990s writing and she is thanked (with reference to The Bible's Rebecca) on the credits of *The Future*. She also directed the video for the single version of 'Closing Time' (depicting a woozy-looking Cohen in a Toronto bar) – which later won a Canadian Juno award for best rock video of 1994.

Recorded in Los Angeles with Jennifer Warnes joining the core of the same band that made *I'm Your Man*, the record's luxuriant sound was a by now familiar one, though Cohen's ever-plummeting vocal range and increasingly grizzled rasp (this despite finally quitting the cigarettes he had smoked on and off for thirty years) imbued his words with an ineffable atmosphere of prophetic foreboding.

The inherent tone of brooding malevolence notwithstanding, the album was another success (platinum, as was *I'm Your Man*, in Canada). The ironically upbeat 'Closing Time' was even a minor radio hit on American FM stations.

Inevitably there was a summer tour to support the new record. With most of the 1988 band reconvened, dates in Scandinavia, southern Europe, West Germany and a marathon trek through Canada unfurled from late April until the beginning of August. There was a rare detour to nine American cities in July to capitalise on his new-found gossip-column-friendly rock-star status there. The tour was well received, and enthusiasm for Cohen was at an all-time high, remarkable considering that, at 58, his voice was reduced to a baleful, lamenting whisper and his stage presence little more animated than that of a grimacing statue.

In October 1993 Cohen was presented with a Governor-General's Performing Arts Award for his contribution to the Canadian arts. This time, he accepted the accolade and spoke with a certain pride about being recognised by the mother country.

Contemporaneously with the album project, Cohen was putting together a collection of his finest poetry and prose work at the behest of Jack McClelland. McClelland & Stewart had been swallowed by a larger company during the 1980s and Cohen, who had never signed a contract as a writer, believing instead in the good faith of the handshake, was forced, against his better judgement, into a written agreement with new publisher Douglas Gibson. The company started asserting itself in a way that Jack McClelland would never have done – insisting that a collection cherry-picked from Cohen's oeuvre had to include new works and an extensive preface. The disagreements rumbled on through the early 1990s until finally a compromise was reached and the collection, entitled *Stranger Music* (a nod to the ill-fated publishing company he had started with Mary Martin all of a quarter-century previously), was eventually published, without a preface or new works, in 1993.

This well-received authorial collection, along with a live album as perfunctory as its title, *Live*, culled from the 1988 and 1993 concerts released in July 1994, seemed to draw a line under Cohen's renaissance period. It was as if his affairs were being put in order so that he could slink off fulfilled, free to embark on a new chapter of his remarkable life.

But the vehicle rolled on regardless. An uninspired version of Ray Charles' 'Born To Lose' appeared on Elton John's mawkish 1993 *Duets* album, with Cohen's voice at its most drain-like. In 1994, two further tribute albums were released, one esoteric, the other pure Tin Pan Alley. The former, *Pa Norsk*, was a collection of nuggets essayed by exclusively female artists from Norway (Cohen would have, no doubt, appreciated the implicit tribute to Marianne). The second, entitled *Tower Of Song*, showcased major rock and pop stars gurning and grandstanding their way through Cohen's finest compositions. Only Willie Nelson's 'Bird On The Wire' and Suzanne Vega's 'Story Of Isaac' emerged without debilitating *faux* gravitas – though Tori Amos's frighteningly psyched 'Famous Blue Raincoat' deserves to be mentioned in dispatches. Despite, or perhaps because of, the overweening schmaltz, the album, essentially the brainchild of Cohen's latest manager Kelley Lynch, sold well, finally securing Cohen's place in the pantheon of rock greats. Lynch, who had worked in Marty Machat's New York office and took over responsibility for Cohen after Machat's 1985 death, saw her role as guarantor of the legend, ensuring his place in the annals and running his Los Angeles office, as she continues to do, with protective, even ruthless efficiency.

In 1995 Jeff Buckley (son of west coast folk eminence Tim) wowed the critics with his debut *Grace* album, the highlight of which was his sumptuous reworking of Cohen's sublime 'Hallelujah', a song whose ancient-sounding gravity enlivened contemporary touring sets by Bob Dylan and John Cale amongst others.

To mark Cohen's sixtieth birthday, a book of tributes entitled *Take This Waltz* was published in Canada, featuring reminiscences and comments from, among others, Judy Collins and Jennifer Warnes. Cohen's last recorded work was undertaken at the close of 1994 when he provided the suitably grave voice for the soundtrack of a filmed version of the Tibetan *Book Of The Dead* (the Dalai Lama also featured).

His public persona thus enshrined, Cohen retired from public life. Since early in 1995 he has devoted himself to the Mount Baldy Zen retreat where he wears monks' robes, shaves his head and lives in an unheated room in a hut containing an electric keyboard, a radio and little else. He seems happy, finally attending to the spiritual dilemmas that have haunted him for most of his adult life. He is not a prisoner: he makes regular trips back down the mountain in a state-of-the-art jeep to his house in Los Angeles. For years he has not been a Buddhist in the strictest sense (he continues to observe Jewish holidays and rituals), his thirst for meditation, not to mention the monastery sake, drawing him into the religion's fold. But in August 1996 Cohen was formerly ordained as a Buddhist monk at the Mount Baldy monastery. His name now is Jikan ('Silent One'). Nevertheless, he keeps on writing (a book and several songs were completed in 1998) and attends to his oeuvre (he chose the tracks for a second hits collection, *More Best Of Leonard Cohen*, released by Sony in 1997).

At a pensionable 66 there appears to be no room for a romantic diversion from his ascetic lifestyle – but appearances can be deceptive when it comes to Cohen's private life. It is not for nothing that in late 1995 he changed the name of his own company from Stranger Music to Bad Monk Publishing.

TWO

THE MUSIC

Songs Of Leonard Cohen

Released: December 1967
Chart position: UK: 13
US: 83
Producer: John Simon
Engineer: uncredited
Recorded: August 1967, Columbia Studio E, New York

> *An assured and unique debut, it immediately estab-*
> *lished the former novelist as a maverick star in the*
> *firmament of late 1960s music – deservedly so.*

Suzanne

Still Cohen's best known song, a gorgeously mellow paean to Montreal artist Suzanne Verdal. Luxuriant Spanish guitar, gossamer girl-harmonies and sombre cellos frame Cohen's gnomic cogitations on his saint-like muse. It's hard to imagine a time when this song didn't exist: it's that good.

Master Song

A dark, chorus-less dissection of a messy *menage à trois* ('Your love is a secret all over the block'), with Cohen's palpable *longueurs* shadowed by burbling double bass and shivers of electric guitar and strings. Wonky singing spoils it.

Winter Lady

Fading in on lilting guitar with flute and distant piano, this is a simple, poignant song – a portrait of Marianne Ihlen (Cohen's Norwegian 'winter lady'), this is perhaps Cohen's least portentous early composition.

The Stranger Song

Dextrous finger-picking distinguishes a 10-verse, minor-key depiction of a failed relationship (an amalgam of Cohen's own romantic impasses), filled with heady imagery ('the highway curls like smoke...just some Joseph looking for a manger'...). It's a bit grim in truth.

Sisters Of Mercy

Written about two back-packing siblings Cohen put up in his hotel room after chancing upon them sheltering from the snow in an Edmonton, Alberta, doorway. Accordion and xylophone create the requisite ambience.

So Long, Marianne

Droning violins, tinny guitars and a stuttering snare-drum create a faux-Cajun feel, into which Cohen's valedictory words effortlessly melt (his affair with Marianne Ihlen was by now, patently, moribund). Keening female backing vocals dominate on the memorable chorus. Being a busker's staple for years has compromised its potency.

Hey, That's No Way To Say Goodbye

A simple, lovely melody, perfectly echoed by pellucid guitar, sees Cohen in exceptionally fine voice, once more sweetening the end of his relationship with somewhat tenuous-sounding optimism. The insouciant, wordless backing vocals are surely a steal from Astrud Gilberto.

Stories Of The Street

Cohen views the world from his bleak room at the Chelsea Hotel and considers his suffering ('One hand on my suicide, the other on the rose') over mechanically strummed chords. Glum and ancient-sounding, it's the darkest song on the record.

Teachers

A relentless minor-chord riff, enlivened by (an uncredited) stringed instrument, possibly a bazouki, sees Cohen intoning over thirteen long verses, with lacerating self-loathing, as he yearns for the necessary wisdom to overcome his depression. Not much fun, really.

One Of Us Cannot Be Wrong

Backed by just his own deft guitar, Cohen picks over another failed relationship. The coda, with his pained screams replacing the resigned lyrics, makes for a disquieting finale.

Songs From A Room

Released: March 1969
Chart position: UK: 2
US: 145
Producer: Bob Johnston
Engineer: Neil Wilburn
Recorded: October 1968, Columbia Studio A, Nashville

Many Cohenites' favourite album, his most successful in the UK. A boon to Jew's harp salesmen the world over.

Bird On The Wire

The paradigm of early Cohen. Lambent guitar, sonorous cello, incongruous Jew's harp and Cohen's voice, small and tortured. The moment when the strings well up on the line, 'I saw a beggar leaning on his wooden crutch', is spine-tingling. A song of independence, inspired by the Greek government's project to bring electricity to Cohen's adopted island home. Timeless and The Neville Brothers did a lovely version. The Beautiful South's wasn't bad either.

Story Of Isaac

The biblical story of Abraham and Isaac used as a device to describe the nature of inter-generational attrition. Ethereal organ and basic guitar establish the eerie ambience. Over-earnest lyrics detract attention from a decent enough tune.

A Bunch Of Lonesome Heroes

'So Long, Marianne' (in rhythm, atmosphere and instrumentation) re-written as the semi-spoken reminiscence of a world-weary soldier. Full rock drums make their first appearance in a Cohen song. Spunky, but not his best.

The Partisan

Cohen's first recorded cover version is a song written during World War II by Anna Marly, who ran a hostel for fleeing French nationals in London. A children's chorus, in French, and shards of accordion capture the appropriate exile's feel. Cohen learned the song from *The People's Songbook* while holidaying in a Quebec summer-camp in 1949. A little perfunctory in its execution.

Seems So Long Ago, Nancy

Skeletal yet transfixing, this homage to his Montreal friend Nancy Becal is a landmark in the Cohen cannon. Bob Johnston's mournful celeste compliments the distracted-sounding singer's nostalgic recollections of the year 1961. A touching and unpretentious *memento mori*.

The Old Revolution

'I finally broke into the prison, I found my place in the chain,' Cohen murmurs in this terse comment on the struggle between rich and poor. A now familiar ensemble of guitar, bass and Jew's harp provide support. The subtext is Cohen's embracing of commercial pop music after his years in thrall to the highbrow literati: 'to all my architects let me now be traitor'.

The Butcher

A drug song. Basic guitar, hallucinatory wordplay and the weariest of vocals render this entirely antithetical to the euphoric narcotic visions being espoused by contemporaries like The Beatles. Dour as a result.

You Know Who I Am

A resigned and extremely bleak treatise on yet another entropic relationship. The first instance of Cohen treading water, this grim vignette is not redeemed even by its lulling waltz-time or spectral organ.

Lady Midnight

Another 3/4 time signature, with bass, guitar, organ and Jew's harp providing the platform for more soul-searching. The relationship in crisis is explored once more – though this time the tone is triumphant ('You've won me, you've won me, my Lord').

Tonight Will Be Fine

A song in standard country-folk form. An adenoidal Cohen describes his Hydra music room and the hovering presence of his lover in the room upstairs ('the soft naked lady'). It's not hard to imagine Johnny Cash singing this, although he might have dispensed with Cohen's tuneless recorder solo.

Songs Of Love And Hate

Released:	September 1971
Chart position:	UK: 4
	US: 63
Producer:	Bob Johnston
Engineer:	uncredited
Recorded:	March 1971, Columbia Studio A, Nashville.

The album that established Cohen's enduring reputation as the suicide's serenader. Provoked comments of the 'you have to turn out the lights to listen to this so you can see the words' ilk from undergraduates the world over. Still terrific though.

Avalanche

Setting the tone for what is a starkly beautiful album, this creeps in on rapid-fire finger-picking and transcendent strings before Cohen's somnolent votive offering to the god of emotional anguish kicks in with untrammelled gloom. Gorgeously wrecked songwriting and a peerless performance.

Last Year's Man

Biblical imagery and choice chords vie with exquisitely sad violins and a genuinely moving children's chorus (recorded in London, at Bob Johnston's behest, the clipped enunciation adding to the evocative incongruity) in Cohen's most vivid portrait of depression ('an hour has gone by and he has not moved his hand'). Ineffably triumphant, despite all the evidence to the contrary.

Dress Rehearsal Rag

Angrily strummed, the embittered verses of this twisted anthem to despondency give way to elegantly resigned choruses ('wasn't it a long way down?'), with Cohen's penchant for razor-blades and suicidal tendencies heavily featured in the barbed, uncompromising lyrics. Genuinely moving.

Diamonds In The Mine

Jaunty and taut, with Charlie Daniels and co providing a country-ish counterpoint to Cohen's reggae-style 12-string pulse. On first hearing this could almost be happy. Its lyrics, dwelling on loneliness and isolation, tell another story. Susan Mussamono and Corlynn Hanney's feisty harmonies enliven Cohen's cracked vocals on the choruses. Oddly sequenced, it rather crassly breaks the carefully established mood. This is a decidedly lesser work.

Love Calls You By Your Name

Revisits 'Avalanche''s picked minor chords and sepulchral musings. Essentially a glimmer of hope (the major-chord choruses) in a sea of doubt (the downbeat verses). Naturally, the latter outweigh the former ten to one.

Famous Blue Raincoat

More benchmark Cohen. Detailing a complex love triangle, this elegant song builds on Cohen's delightful guitar figure and auto-biographical, cinematic scene-setting ('It's four in the morning, the end of December'). Susan Mussammono's operatic descant is a joy in itself. Gorgeous and unique.

Sing Another Song, Boys

Rather superfluous (and again exploding the somnolent mood of its predecessors) this brazen live take from the 1970 Isle Of Wight Festival develops from an uncertain start to a fulminating climax – with Bob Johnston's churchy organ much in evidence. You'd never guess it was recorded at 4am, such is its zest.

Joan Of Arc

Cohen's love token to Nico. Using a device (its name borrowed from literature), the palimpsest, wherein one spoken vocal is shadowed by an over-dubbed sung version – this is a quiet and pretty song with contrastingly libidinous, voyeuristic lyrics (about sating his 'swollen appetite'). Arch and overweening, it's Cohen at his least subtle. No wonder she turned him down.

Live Songs

Released:	April 1973
Chart position:	UK: –
	US: –
Producer:	Bob Johnston
Engineer:	Bob Potter
Recorded:	in London, Brussels, Berlin, Paris and The Isle Of Wight on tours in 1970 and 1972 and in late '72 at home in Tennessee.

Perfunctory live epistle – more interesting document than essential addition to the canon.

Minute Prologue
Cohen extemporising about the healing power of song, over rudimentary guitar. Recorded at the Royal Albert Hall in 1972. Ephemeral.

Passin' Thru
A great singalong country standard (written by one Richard Blakeslee) given a fairly straight reading, with Cohen doing his best Hank Williams whine.

You Know Who I Am
A sombre take on an already sombre song, with minor lyrical adjustments and lovely backing vocals from Jennifer Warnes ('Warren' in the credits).

Bird On The Wire
Presaged by a French translation of the song's chorus, an effortlessly lovely version of the *Songs From A Room* prototype.

Seems So Long Ago, Nancy
Credited simply as 'Nancy', this is, again, a lyrically revised, though otherwise faithful, recapitulation of the studio original. Fabulous, in other words.

Improvisation
With Cohen's Spanish guitar chords at the helm, guitarists Ron Cornelius and David O'Conner extemporise around the introduction to 'You Know Who I Am' to somewhat aimless effect.

Story Of Isaac
Introduced as 'a song about those who would sacrifice one generation on behalf of another', the song works perfectly thus re-cast as an anti-Vietnam war protest.

Please Don't Pass Me By (A Disgrace)
The otherwise unrecorded 13-minute long parable of the blind New York beggar Cohen spied wearing a placard with the above title written on it. Part rapped, part sung (with a certain tone-deaf *brio*) this features entirely inappropriate clap-along audience participation. Splendid song nonetheless.

Tonight Will Be Fine
From the Isle Of Wight show this is a rollicking, even optimistic version of the *Songs From A Room* closer – with Charlie Daniels's unfettered fiddle leading the line.

Queen Victoria
A dour ordeal of a song (just a fuzzy-voiced Cohen and two-chord guitar) recorded in the singer's Tennessee cabin – with references to his father and events from his childhood, it is an unremarkable work which nevertheless made *Live Songs* essential for Cohen completists. Superfluous for most, though.

Leonard Cohen: for many the epitome of the louche bohemian poet, for others synonymous with one word: depression.

Above and right Despite not taking the stage until a wearying 4.00am at the Isle of Wight Festival in 1970, Cohen was universally hailed as the star of the show.

Above Despite his own reservations, Cohen's live performances were often awe-inspiring.
Below Cohen was capable of making even a walk in the park a depressing experience.

Left A pensive Cohen ponders on yet another tiresome live performance while the photographer looks on.

Above Cohen at the time of 1977's Phil Spector-produced curio *Death of a Ladies' Man.*

Left The success of Cohen's 1988 collaboration with Jennifer Warnes on 'Famous Blue Raincoat' and his own *I'm Your Man* brought financial security and was the closest he ever got to real pop-star status.

Above By the early 1990s, a more dapper-looking Cohen was at ease both with the press and with himself.

Above and right In this 1995 photo session Cohen seemed relaxed and happy, in readiness for moving into the next chapter of his life as a Buddhist monk.

New Skin For The Old Ceremony

Released: July 1974
Chart position: UK 24
US –
Producers: John Lissauer and Leonard Cohen
Engineers: Rick Rowe and Frank Laico
Recorded: February 1974, Columbia Studio A, New York

> *A lesser album in the Cohen catalogue, but also one of his least unctuous and not without its moments of transcendence. The sleeve illustration dates from 1550.*

Is This What You Wanted

A terse yet lamenting tribute to Cohen's crumbling relationship with Suzanne Elrod ('you got old and wrinkled, I stayed 17'). The staccato chorus comes as something of a shock (the complicated drums are by Roy Markowitz) – with Cohen coolly laconic at first, desperate and discordant by the close. Cohen carries off this revision to his established style with great panache.

Chelsea Hotel

Cohen's infamous tribute to Janis Joplin and the wild bohemian days of New York in the late 1960s. Unstinting in its detail ('giving me head on the un-made bed…') this is deliciously mournful and nostalgic, with elegant guitar and funereal horns. Rightly, one of Cohen's most celebrated compositions.

Lover, Lover, Lover

Catchy and uptempo (with that rare Cohen commodity: a euphoric, singalong chorus) with spirited percussion and liminal backing vocals from Erin Dickens and Emily Bindinger. It was later recorded by Echo & The Bunnymen. Cohen's version is the better.

Field Commander Cohen
Wordy, multi-paced and deeply autobiographical (Cohen depicts himself as 'the patron saint of envy and the grocer of despair'), this is a suite of disparate musical elements glued together by Cohen's excellent close-mic'd, almost conversational vocals.

Why Don't You Try
Smoky and confessional, with jazzy double bass by Don Payne and clipped mandolin by Jeff Layton, Cohen the torch singer sounds confident and unusually mellifluous.

There Is A War
Using the hackneyed metaphor of the battlefield, Cohen dwells on the volatile chasm between man and woman. Again in fine voice, the suitably melodramatic atmosphere comes courtesy of Lewis Furey's viola. Some way from being his most memorable tune, all the same.

A Singer Must Die
A courtroom drama with a self-mocking Cohen on trial for betraying his art (for 'the lie in his voice'). The eloquent lyrics sit snugly amid doleful woodwind. A clever song.

I Tried To Leave You
Self-explanatory dissection of his 'marital' affairs ('I closed the book on us a hundred times'). A grimly real, almost jazzy torch song with simple guitar and rich bass.

Who By Fire
Classic Cohen. Biblical of word and strong in melody, John Lissauer's

semi-classical arrangement for viola and percussion provides the perfect ascetic foil for some trenchant musing on mortality. It's one of Cohen's most economical compositions – and perhaps the catchiest.

Take This Longing

Another song written with Nico in mind (it had been gestating since 1966). Cohen's rejection by the German chanteuse clearly still rankled ('your body like a searchlight, my poverty revealed'). Beautifully written and, for all its mordant self-deprecation, carefully rendered.

Leaving Green Sleeves

Composed around the skeleton of the 16th-century folk song (apocryphally credited to Henry VIII) of the same name, Cohen, in mock-arcane language, rakes over the leaves of his ruined love life to the tune of a rippling harpsichord. If any Cohen song could be dismissed as throwaway, this is it.

Death Of A Ladies' Man

Released: November 1977
Chart position: UK: 35
US: –
Producer: Phil Spector
Engineer: Larry Levine
Recorded: June–July 1977, Gold Star, Whitney Recording and Devonshire Sound Studios, Los Angeles.

An oddball collaboration, much pilloried at the time, now rightly revered as a classically strange hybrid. All songs credited to Spector/Cohen.

True Love Leaves No Traces
For Cohen aficionados the shock of hearing Spector's clamorous easy listening arrangement, with their man's vocals buried about a mile back in the mix, is incalculable. A lazy, swooning melodic backdrop, rich in flutes, makes a fabulously incongruous setting for Cohen's elegiac essay on lost love. Lovely, for all its oddness.

Iodine
Two drummers (Hal Blaine and Jim Keltner) propel this saxophone-encrusted rock 'n' roll ballad, with Ronee Blakely's meandering harmonies rendering Cohen all but inaudible as he distantly barks his 'masquerade of trust'. Opulent-sounding, despite the mismatch.

Paper Thin Hotel
Plangent and cinemascopic, Cohen's voyeuristic motel memoir gets the full (decidedly *not* paper-thin) wall-of-sound treatment. More Neil Diamond in style, it is, nonetheless, a classic Cohen analysis of sexual longing. Spector's production grandeur really adds to the lyrical claustrophobia.

Memories
Inspired by nostalgia for his high-school prom ('Frankie Laine was singing Jezebel') and memories of lusting – yet again – after Nico ('the tallest and the blondest girl'), this is a cavernous, *faux* doo-wop anthem with a 10-strong backing choir doing their utmost to obliterate Cohen's impassioned mewlings. Bizarrely affecting.

I Left A Woman Waiting
More nostalgia, more phalanxes of flute and saxophone. At least Cohen is audible in this picaresque tale of lost beauty, regret and the redeeming spiritual qualities of sexual congress. The album's least successful fusion of styles.

Don't Go Home With Your Hard-On

Gospel music *sans* religion. In its place, sexual frustration. Massed drummers, phased guitars and Allen Ginsberg and Bob Dylan on backing vocals power this rich, sardonic juggernaut, a veritable Wagnerian hymn to unconsummated love. Breathtaking.

Fingerprints

Unreconstructed country music on the surface, on closer inspection a confession to sexual guilt. Bobby Bruce's fiddle and 'Sneaky' Pete Kleinow's pedal-steel guitar provide the former, a reverb-soaked Cohen the latter. Forgettable, ultimately.

Death Of A Ladies' Man

Deathly slow and shrouded in strings and synthesizers, Cohen, thankfully given some breathing space in the continent-wide mix, essays an affectingly vexed-sounding performance to voice the *longueurs* of a lapsed lothario. A sad and swooning nine-minute swansong.

Recent Songs

Released: September 1979
Chart position: UK: 53
US: –
Producer: Leonard Cohen, Henry Lewry
Engineer: Skip Cottrell
Recorded: April–May 1979, A&M studios, Los Angeles.

Returns Cohen to more intimate musical surroundings, with jazz and Eastern influences threaded throughout.

The Guests

Graceful if lachrymose, with Jennifer Warnes showing off her celestial pipes and Raffi Hakopian's Arabic-flavoured violin much in evidence. Cohen cleverly reverses his initial observations about the 'open-hearted many, the broken-hearted few', at the close.

Humbled By Love

Jazzy and cool, with Roscoe Beck's double-bass and Mitch Watkins's guitar setting the smoky tone, while Cohen gradually shakes off a broken heart in favour of celebratory savouring ('I will never hold a woman this close'). Cohen is right on top of his game here.

The Window

Ineffably Middle-Eastern-sounding and full of remorse. Ed Lustgarden's cello and Hakopian's violin provide the suitably morose chamber music setting.

Came So Far For Beauty

An autobiographical piano ballad which wouldn't seem out of place on a Randy Newman album. Co-author John Lissauer caresses the ivories deftly, and Johnny Miller plucks elastic bass, over which Cohen coos with languid tristesse. Essentially a manifesto for the Cohen sensibility, it's a truly lovely song.

The Lost Canadian (*Un Canadien Errant*)

Sung in French, this is a 19th-century folk song written by M.A. Gerin-Lajoie about an exiled soldier. It's an understandable choice for the itinerant poet-combatant; the inappropriately insouciant Mexican mariachi combo accompaniment is, however, slightly more baffling.

The Traitor

Caressed by a lilting chamber ensemble (organ, strings, oud) this returns Cohen to the mood of his early albums. The title refers to the author's reputation for 'selective' monogamy. The beautiful musicianship cannot save a dull tune.

Our Lady Of Solitude
A tribute to the personification of love Cohen finds in an unnamed lover ('all summer long she touched me'), that floats on Band mainstay Garth Hudson's sublime synthesizer chords. Happy, upbeat and, at just over three minutes, very much to the point.

The Gypsy's Wife
Ostensibly an observation on the last days of Cohen's relationship with Suzanne Elrod, this is a treatise on the incompatibility of men and women in general, essayed with skilful economy over some gorgeous minor chords.

The Smokey Life
Less agonising than much of the album, this resides on a bed of Fender Rhodes piano (courtesy of Bill Ginn), with a lazy swinging rhythm and precise duetting from Jennifer Warnes. A lovely chorus melody recalls Joni Mitchell.

Ballad Of The Absent Mare
A 12-verse allegory about a cowboy and his wayward steed. The lyrics are based on an early Chinese poem (about an ox-herder) which, with the mariachi band this time gainfully employed, provides a gently optimistic, if a tad overlong, *denouement*.

Various Positions

Released: June 1984
Chart position: UK: 52
US: not released
Producer: John Lissauer
Engineer: Leanne Ungar
Recorded: February 1984, Quadrasonic Sound studio,
New York

Cohen begins to embrace the technology of the studio. CBS New York don't get it at all, Cohen's European fans do.

Dance Me To The End Of Love

Electronic keyboards and a drum machine usher in the Cohen '80s. Jennifer Warnes's cooing vocals and a la-la-la theme, part Hasidic lament, part Eurovision Song Contest, link into the past. Irrepressible and charming stuff, this is one of Cohen's finest recorded moments.

Coming Back To You

A piano-heavy, country-ish ballad – a mood enforced by Sid McGinnes' twanging guitar. A tissue-soft soundscape makes a perfectly virginal canvas for Cohen's grizzled resignation.

The Law

A grave little song with a claustrophobic sound, reggae-ish beat and gliding harmonies into which Cohen inserts his meditation on a womaniser's life ('my heart's like a blister from doing what I do'). Seriously dark.

Night Comes On
With Jennifer Warnes singing a meticulous counterpoint throughout, Cohen addresses his life chronologically, with slide guitar and familiar Spanish six-string leavening the luminescent pools of synthesizer and Fender Rhodes. Touching.

Hallelujah
Hymnal and graceful, this, once again Biblically-themed *tour de force* is one of Cohen's most perfectly realised epistles. With sparse accompaniment (mainly synthetic bass and drums), Cohen and Warnes carry the euphonious tune with suitably celestial vigour. A song that's impossible to perform without bringing a lump to the throat, as John Cale and Jeff Buckley (if he were still with us) would attest. Timeless and peerless quasi-religious songwriting.

The Captain
A conversation between a raw recruit and his commanding officer set to a foot-tapping country rag. A black sense of humour pervades the lyrics ('there is no decent place to stand in a massacre'). Sprightly and wry.

Hunter's Lullaby
A return to an earlier sound. The stripped-down, folky setting can't disguise a mawkish tune and Cohen's inability to carry the simple melody. It seems, incredibly, to be in a key too deep for him.

Heart With No Companion
Another makeweight. A rudimentary country tune (replete with square-dance fiddle and clichéd harmonica) finds Cohen swimming in bathos to negligible effect.

If It Be Your Will

The album's most affecting song. Again Cohen's guitar and tone of humility (not to mention Warnes' gorgeous ululations) distinguish this serene spiritual incantation. It sounds like it was recorded in a church, such is the reverent atmosphere conjured by every carefully enunciated syllable and every teased guitar note.

I'm Your Man

Released:	February 1988
Chart position:	UK: 48
	US: –
Producers:	Leonard Cohen, Roscoe Beck, Jean-Phillippe Rykiel, Michel Robidoux
Engineers:	Ian Terry, Jean-Jacques Peruchon, Leanne Ungar.
Recorded:	August-November 1987, Studio Tempo, Montreal; Soundworks, New York; Ragg Street and Rock Steady studios, Los Angeles.

The album that returned Cohen to the centre stage, his reinvention as an avuncular sage in a Gucci two-piece, endearing him to a new generation of fans.

First We Take Manhattan

Menacing and electronic, this launched Cohen on his synthetic odyssey into the MTV heartland. Apocalyptic in tone yet smart and modern, it proved his sense of musical acuity was as keen as his basement voice was shot. The song's narrator was meant to be insane, by the way.

Ain't No Cure For Love
Cohen's prognostications on the timeless lure of physical desire, inspired by the ramifications of the AIDS virus. The cop-show saxophone theme and pulsing sequencers can't disguise the misgivings implicit in the lyrics ('I've got you like a habit'). A wonderful, galloping song with few precedents.

Everybody Knows
A wry, quasi-disco-grooved pop tune, written with singer Sharon Robinson. Cohen's voice is at its barrel-scraping lowest and John Bilezikjian's oud at its most exotic. Surely an influence on Bob Dylan's similarly themed 'Everything Is Broken', written the same year.

I'm Your Man
Tinny drum machine and kitsch synthesiser open this mordantly funny self-portrait. A bruised, seedy vocal dominates the elevator music backing. Exquisitely delivered and irresistibly charming.

Take This Waltz
A waltz, unsurprisingly, re-mixed from a track on the 1986 Lorca tribute LP *Poetas En Nueva York*. The main addition to that is a wonderfully fluid violin part by Raffi Hakopian. Elegant to a fault.

Jazz Police
An unsuccessful attempt at angular electro-pop. Apparently inspired by his band's efforts to get Cohen to play more complicated chords. Ironic, Orwellian lyrics get lost in the synthetic bluster. Nice idea, but overcooked.

I Can't Forget
Luxuriant pop, replete with loquacious marimbas and airy keyboards. Cohen sounds taut and edgy ('I smoked a cigarette and tightened up

my gut') as he plans a mysterious rendezvous in Phoenix, Arizona. A
minor diversion.

Tower Of Song

Cohen at his most alluringly lugubrious ('I ache in the places where I
used to play') as he assesses his life in love and music. A tribute, of
sorts, to Hank Williams, it also features Cohen's first recorded (and
frankly autistic-sounding) keyboard solo. A marvellous achievement in
that it welds humour to poignancy with effortless ease. 12-bar blues
at its most unusual.

The Future

Released:	November 1992
Chart position:	UK: 36
	US: –
Producers:	Leonard Cohen, Steve Lindsey, Bill Ginn,
	Leanne Ungar, Rebecca De Mornay, Yoav Green
Engineer:	Leanne Ungar
Recorded:	throughout the first six months of 1992 at Image
	Recording, The Complex, Mad Hatter, Studio 56,
	House Of Soul, Village Recorder, Capitol Recording
	and Cherokee studios, Los Angeles.

*Handicapped by an over-glossy production and Cohen's
moribund vocal cords, this, nonetheless, picks up the
sardonic baton from* I'm Your Man *and runs with it.*

The Future
Cohen's dystopian prophecy set to a pulsating rock-lite backing. He is in unequivocal mood ('give me crack and anal sex') and has no time for compassion ('all the little poets coming round trying to sound like Charlie Manson'). Quite disturbing.

Waiting For The Miracle
Another Sharon Robinson collaboration. Anjani Thomas's vocal wraps around Cohen's choked bark as limpid synthesizer chords float over a lolling drum machine. The miracle could just be the couple of octaves missing from Cohen's vocal range.

Be For Real
A cover of Frederick Knight's 1970s soul classic. Possibly the line, 'If it's a thrill you're looking for, well honey, I'm flexible', is what attracted Cohen to the song. He certainly sings it with deadpan sincerity (and sounds not unlike Barry White). Filler, ultimately.

Closing Time
Catchy and up-tempo with Bob Furgo's hoedown fiddle to the fore, this is, nonetheless, a studious contemplation of mortality. Fortunately only Cohen's voice is six feet under. Country music with a brain.

Anthem
Co-arranged and nominally produced by Rebecca De Mornay, this is MOR with a touch of the biblical ('There's a crack in everything – that's where the light gets in'). The LA Mass Choir shield Cohen's hoarse, broken vocals. It's difficult not to be seduced by the wondrous atmosphere of this huge-sounding production.

Democracy

Whittled down from 80 verses to a mere seven, this is Cohen's *fin-de-siècle* treatise on salvation. Using America as a template, he predicts a time, in contrast to the sentiments expressed in *The Future*, when inequalities will be eradicated. Vinnie Colaiuta's military drums and Jennifer Warnes' glacial harmonies help make the point with stentorian brio. A great monolith of a song.

Light As The Breeze

A slow, aching ballad in which Cohen sounds ancient and exhausted, an arthritic Don Juan, feeling the ice in his joints melted by another new love whom he is only too happy to 'pleasure'. Witty and brave songwriting.

Always

Irving Berlin's 1925 love pledge given a torpid R&B make-over. Cohen seems disinterested and leaves it to the 'angels' to do the tune while the band indulge in a litany of pointless solos. Unlovely.

Tacoma Trailer

Originally composed for a now-forgotten theatrical production, this is an atmospheric six-minute coda in the style of Erik Satie, on which Cohen doesn't even appear (Bill Ginn does the honours on piano). It really doesn't belong here.

Leonard Cohen – Live In Concert

Released: July 1994
Chart position: UK: 35
US: –
Producers: Leanne Ungar, Bob Metzger
Engineers: Alan Perman, Leanne Ungar
Recorded: On tour in 1988 and 1993 in Toronto,
San Sebastian, Amsterdam, Austin and Vancouver.

A curate's egg. Some tender interpretations compete with bland reworkings. Still an accurate record of the last days of Cohen's singing voice.

Dance Me To The End Of Love
Rapturous Torontonian applause greets the opening bars of this curtain-raiser (with Cohen's clumsy keyboard ad-libs). It`s a pretty faithful rendering, with lovely violin from Bob Furgo.

Bird On The Wire
A funeral-paced take on a Cohen classic. His borderline-baritone croak eradicates any trace of melody but there's a certain poignant charm about his karaoke-style attempt, nonetheless.

Everybody Knows
The voice is subterranean but the band is propulsive and watertight. Some subtle lyrical adjustments ('sacred heart' becomes 'mighty heart') make it a target for the train-spotters (pain-spotters?). Hard to do a song this good badly.

Joan Of Arc
Deathly slow and re-cast as a call-and-response with backing vocalist

87

Julie Christensen. Rather perfunctory-sounding all the same.

There Is A War
Made over from its 1974 incarnation as a clipped soul groove, and effectively so.

Sisters Of Mercy
Cohen at the guitar and in reasonable voice – the backing singers are also in 'angelic' form. A truly beautiful song.

Hallelujah
A snail's-pace version of the *Various Positions* highlight. The prayer-like chorus is just as moving at half speed, and Cohen's phrasing is on the money throughout.

I'm Your Man
More wry lyrical revisions ('I'll wear a leather mask for you') invite amused applause from a hip Toronto audience. Spirited and sardonic, this is an obvious live winner.

Who By Fire
A terrific version. Cohen seems to have discovered a lost octave (it's from an Austin show in 1988, possibly the last time Cohen exhibited anything like a vocal range).

One Of Us Cannot Be Wrong
MOR rock serves one of Cohen's earliest compositions well. Again the singing is croak-free and the band a well-oiled machine.

If It Be Your Will
Cohen alone (for the most part) with his guitar. Sombre, intimate and

magnificent, this even eclipses the recorded version. Rather than merely extolling God, Cohen sounds like God. Utterly wonderful.

Heart With No Compassion
Jaunty and almost impossible to dislike in its guise as a bravura country-rock toe-tapper.

Suzanne
Full circle. The first and the last track in Cohen's recorded oeuvre to date. His guitar (detuned a whole tone to accommodate the crippled larynx) twangs and the familiar melody unfurls like dark smoke. A true classic.

OTHER ALBUMS:

Greatest Hits (US: Best Of Leonard Cohen)

Released: November 1975
Tracks: Suzanne/Sisters Of Mercy/So Long, Marianne/
Bird On The Wire/Lady Midnight/The Partisan/
Hey, That's No Way To Say Goodbye/Famous Blue
Raincoat/Last Year's Man/Chelsea Hotel No.2/
Who By Fire/Take This Longing

Cohen In Warsaw

Released: (on cassette, only in Poland) 1985

Six Montreal Poets (eight poems)

Released: Folkways, 1957

Canadian Poets 1 (7 poems)

Released: CBS Canada, 1966

Greatest Hits Volume 2

Released: Columbia, 1997

TRIBUTE ALBUMS

Famous Blue Raincoat

Cypress, 1987

Jennifer Warnes sang her favourite songs written by her favourite employer. Did more for his career than for hers.

First We Take Manhattan/Bird On The Wire/Famous Blue Raincoat/ Joan Of Arc/Ain't No Cure For Love/Coming Back To You/Song Of Bernadette/A Singer Must Die/Came So Far For Beauty
Cohen duets on Joan Of Arc

I'm Your Fan: The Songs Of Leonard Cohen

Released: September 1991
Chart position: UK: –
USA: –
Producer: Various
Engineer: Various
Recorded: Summer 1991 in various locations.

French-sourced tribute which capitalised on the success of I'm Your Man and introduced Cohen to a new generation of fans. The indie rock fraternity do their best to bludgeon most of the subtleties from the songs but the durability of Cohen's songwriting survives all but the most banal assault.

The House Of Love: Who By Fire

Singer Guy Chadwick's muted monotone, naturally sharing Cohen's limited baritone range, sits comfortably at the centre of this gently clipped acoustic rendering. Oddly, they manage to make it sound like they wrote it.

Ian McCulloch: Hey, That's No Way To Say Goodbye

Arch Cohen fan and Echo & The Bunnymen leader McCulloch obviously loves the catchy ones (he's also reprised 'Lover, Lover, Lover'), and he manages a fairly faithful rendition here. His vocal is a tad melodramatic and the rocky backing unexceptional but it's a difficult song to do badly. He doesn't.

Pixies: I Can't Forget

A brave choice – as you might expect from lead Pixie Black Francis (later Frank Black). Unfortunately it's a plodding, fuzzy guitar-riven and unwieldy attempt, despite Warnes-like harmonies from Kim Deal. We can forget.

That Petrol Emotion: Stories Of The Street

An unlikely success given the band's propensity for garage-rock/dance hybrids and singer Steve Mack's sugary vocals. Here he is plaintive and sensitive while the band are untypically understated to a fault with Joe Doherty's viola and Steve Anstee's cello much in evidence.

The Lilac Time: Bird On The Wire

Lead Lilac Steven Duffy's winsome warbling and clunking banjo never quite get to grips with the hymnal qualities of Cohen's most lonesome epistle, re-casting it instead as the mild ennui of a Midlands schoolboy procrastinating over his Sunday night homework. Lightweight.

Geoffrey Oryema: Suzanne

On paper, an inspired choice. Paris-based Ugandan Oryema might have been expected to recast Cohen's loveliest song with at least a nod to African music. Instead he essays it like a dull facsimile of the original. A faltering voice and some superfluous percussion don't help. The brief Swahili extemporisation over the fade can't redeem it.

James: So Long, Marianne

It's surprising – given that James were gathering steam as purveyors of pop-rock anthemicism – that this fails to tease out the prototype's gregarious hooks. Tim Booth sings with suitably valedictory gusto (adding some improvised lyrics at the end) and the band clatter away behind him to reasonable effect (Andy Diagram's trumpets are decidedly sanguine on the choruses), but it's ultimately less than the sum of its parts.

Jean-Louis Murat: Avalanche IV

Cohen's bleak existential masterpiece made over as dreary cruise-ship rock-lite. Murat's French translation gives the treatment a soupçon of intrigue but his wafer-thin voice and Aix-en-Provence's blandest session journeymen (plus Prefab Sprout's Neil Conti on drums) render it instantly forgettable. A crime.

David McComb & Adam Peters: Don't Go Home With Your Hard-On

Triffids mainman McComb and cello-wielding sidekick Peters nearly succeed in making over this most pugnaciously ribald essay as a bizarre hip-hop/rock mutant. Taking elements from I'm Your Man's sonic blueprint, the duo shovel sediments of keyboard and phalanxes of twangsome guitar onto a flittering sequencer rhythm and stentorian beats, then turn everything up to eleven. The late David McComb was a dramatic and evocative singer and he handles this with typically angular aplomb.

REM: First We Take Manhattan

Mike Mills on Hammond organ, bass and harmonies (he does the 'angels' bits) steals the show from singer Michael Stipe, who seems to be going through the motions, despite his double-tracked vocals throughout. Nevertheless, Bill Berry's big drums and Peter Buck's rudimentary guitar keep things ticking over while Mills does all the hard stuff. Workmanlike.

Lloyd Cole: Chelsea Hotel

Perfunctory country-rock does this audaciously brilliant song a grave injustice. Robert Quine, usually the most adventurous of guitarists, turns in a performance of Holiday Inn mediocrity and Cole's Dylanesque harp solo is about as individualistic as this dull treatment gets.

Robert Forster: Tower Of Song

Ex-Go-Between Forster is a wry performer and the sardonic flavour of Cohen's cryptic blues is perfectly suited to his declamatory style. The all-German band provide an unobtrusive sub-Velvet Underground backing and Forster carries it all off with great, if not strictly in tune alacrity.

Peter Astor: Take This Longing

One-time Creation Records stalwart Astor had made his name as an exponent of classic underground rock stylings, and Cohen's material is clearly food and drink to him. Daring to reinvent this as a dreamy drum-machine and floating synthesiser paean pays off. Heidi Berry's harmonies are beautifully ethereal and the whole thing drifts by quite charmingly.

Dead Famous People: True Love Leaves No Traces

Produced and engineered by one Serge Gainsbourg, this is a bold attempt at a song that is immutably wedded to the production extravaganza Phil Spector applied to the original. Biddy Leyland's various keyboards do their best to replicate Spector's brass and string armies, but it's a hopeless task, one that even Donna Savage's spirited vocals cannot rescue.

Bill Pritchard: I'm Your Man

Sensitive singer-songwriter Pritchard (English but big, at the time, in France) makes a reasonable job of Cohen's barbed love letter. Dick Lee's saxophone and Foss Paterson's keyboards ape the original and Pritchard's reedy but serviceable pipes carry the tune with some brio. Cohen's exquisite timing is all that's missing.

Fatima Mansions: A Singer Must Die

A fine choice for the notoriously self-lacerating Mansions singer Cathal Coughlan to make. The backing is somewhat transparent and over-reliant on Aindrias O'Gruama's cheesy guitar sounds, but Coughlan sounds convincingly repentant and makes the song his own.

Nick Cave & The Bad Seeds: Tower Of Song

Allegedly a good half-dozen versions of this were recorded with Cave and band in increasing states of inebriation, so much so that they never got to the end of a single one. Instead engineer Victor Van Vugt edited portions of the various takes together to make this patchwork a decidedly leaning tower of song(s). Eerie faux-rockabilly, dysfunctional blues and tuneless caterwauling all vie for dominance as a result. Strangely perplexing.

John Cale: Hallelujah

The album's highlight without a doubt. A relief after all those scratchy electric guitars; Cale's wholly solo voice and piano rendition wrestles every last nuance of gravity from what is already a work of magisterial splendour. The great Welsh polymath has both the larynx and the sensitivity for the job and turns in a performance of heartbreaking poignancy that dares the listener to remain dry-eyed.

Tower Of Song: The Songs Of Leonard Cohen

Released: 1995
Chart position: UK: –
USA: –
Producer: Various
Engineer: Various
Recorded: 1994–95 in various locations.

Frequently-misfiring big name compilation with hysterical sleevenotes by Tom Robbins: 'As society staggers toward the millennium, flailing and screeching all the while, like an orang-utan with a steak knife in its side'. Cheers, Tom. Ultimately, it felt like a cynical attempt to build on I'm Your Fan's good work (hence its identical sub-title), but with some more famous names. A Cohen footnote.

Don Henley: Everybody Knows
Desperately flat.

Trisha Yearwood: Coming Back To You
Cohen often said he was a country singer at heart. A proper country singer simply proved his point. Delicious.

Sting & The Chieftains: Sisters Of Mercy
Sting on autopilot. The Chieftains are simply inappropriate.

Bono: Hallelujah
Bono mutters his way through the lyrics. Louise McCormick screeches in the background and Jeremy Shaw adds some plinky keyboards. Not, actually, very good.

Tori Amos: Famous Blue Raincoat
Just her and her piano. Slow and brooding in the manner of her 'Smells Like Teen Spirit' cover. Almost seems likely to break into Leo Sayer's 'When I Need You'. Lovely.

Aaron Neville: Ain't No Cure For Love
Nice voice, goonish country backing.

Elton John: I'm Your Man
Oh no you're not.

Willie Nelson: Bird On The Wire
Where Cohen's voice is deep, Nelson's is more highly pitched, yet both carry a curiously similar emotional punch. 'Bird On The Wire' is taken at funereal pace. Beautiful.

Peter Gabriel: Suzanne

Similarly paced to Nelson's tune, but without any kind of emotional connection, save the fervent hope that Gabriel clears his throat.

Billy Joel: Light As The Breeze

More funereal pacing. Joel doesn't sound as if he knows it's about cunnilingus.

Jann Arden: If It Be Your Will

Cohen's fellow Canadian Jann Arden's voice is crystal clear, but singing the song as a dirge helps no one despite the presence of Cohen's occasional studio drummer Vinnie Colaiuta.

Suzanne Vega: Story Of Isaac

Cohen's closest female equivalalent. Like Cohen, she understands menace and sexual tension. 'Story Of Isaac' isn't quite the right song for her, but she gives it a fair spin for its money.

Martin Gore: Coming Back For More

Depeche Mode's songwriter and keyboardist blooms with unexpected grace here. His voice has the wonky pathos a Cohen song needs and his piano the instrumental dignity. The closest version here in scope and ambition to the best of I'm Your Fan.

OTHER RECORDINGS

Isle Of Wight/Atlanta 1970

Includes 'Tonight Will Be Fine', CBS, 1971

Earl Scruggs Review Anniversary Special, Vol 1

Includes 'Passin' Thru', CBS, 1975

Are You Okay?

Was (Not Was), Fontana 1990
Cohen sings lead on Elvis's 'Rolls Royce'

Weird Nightmare

Tribute LP to Charlie Mingus, Sony 1992
Cohen does the voiceover on 'Chill Of Death'

Duets

Elton John and various accomplices, Rocket 1993
Cohen duets on 'Born To Lose'

SINGLES

Suzanne/So Long, Marianne – March 1968
Bird On The Wire/Seems So Long Ago, Nancy – May 1969
Joan Of Arc/Diamonds In The Mine – July 1971
Suzanne/Bird On The Wire – March 1973
Bird On The Wire (live)/Tonight Will Be Fine (live) – July 1974
Lover, Lover, Lover/Who By Fire – November 1974
Suzanne/Take This Longing – May 1976
Do I Have To Dance All Night? (live)/The Butcher (live) (France and Portugal only) – July 1976
Memories/Don't Go Home With Your Hard-On – November 1977
True Love Leaves No Traces/I Left A Woman Waiting – March 1978
Dance Me To The End Of Love/The Law – February 1985
Take This Waltz (version of the poem 'Pequeño Vals Vienes' extracted from the Lorca tribute album *Poetas En Nueva York* – single released in Spain and Holland only) – June 1986
First We Take Manhattan/Sisters Of Mercy – January 1988
Ain't No Cure For Love/Jazz Police – May 1988
Closing Time/Anthem – January 1993

EPs (AND 12' SINGLES MARKED*)

Sisters Of Mercy/Winter Lady/The Stranger Song – July 1972
Bird On The Wire/Lady Midnight/Joan Of Arc/Suzanne/Hey, That's No Way To Say Goodbye/So Long, Marianne/Paper Thin Hotel – July 1983 (on Picnick, Europe only)

First We Take Manhattan/Sisters Of Mercy/Bird On The Wire/
Suzanne – January 1988*
Ain't No Cure For Love/Jazz Police/Hey, That's No Way To Say
Goodbye/So Long, Marianne – May 1988*

OTHER WORKS

Poetry

Let Us Compare Mythologies – McGill Poetry Series, 1956
The Spice-Box Of Earth – McClelland & Stewart, 1961
Flowers For Hitler – McClelland & Stewart, 1964
Parasites Of Heaven – McClelland & Stewart, 1966
Selected Poems: 1956–1968 – McClelland & Stewart, 1968
Death Of A Lady's Man – McClelland & Stewart, 1978
Book Of Mercy – McClelland & Stewart, 1984
Stranger Music: Selected Poems & Songs – McClelland & Stewart, 1993

Novels

The Favourite Game – Viking, 1963
Beautiful Losers – McClelland & Stewart, 1966

THREE

THE LEGACY

There are many public perceptions about Leonard Cohen. He is the epitome of the louche bohemian poet to some, for others a spiritually questing, Dylan-esque troubadour, and for many more an enduringly wordy icon of the 1960s counter-cultural revolution. While these are all resonant facets of the Cohen phenomenon, his public persona is defined not by his literary eminence or his place in the post-Woodstock pantheon but, instead, by one lingering and pervasive characteristic. For a conjunction of the word 'Leonard' with the word 'Cohen' is, for the uninitiated at least, synonymous with one thing only: depression.

His, so the consensus has it, is an art obsessed with mental anguish – in particular, his own. Close behind comes the commonly stated rubric that exposure to his material will instantly instil in the listener a similarly morose mental state. His is 'music to slit your wrists by', as the melodramatic platitude goes.

It's not altogether difficult to see why. Cohen's deeply autobiographical, surreally evocative lyrics, almost without exception in the songs that established his name as a force in music, are undeniably bleak depictions of the torments of love and the fragility of the human spirit.

Not that this is a unique concern for a popular singer. Among the many precedents one could cherry-pick any number of blues artists from Robert Johnson onwards, whose wrecked personal affairs and desperate pleas for redemption are played out in starkly chiselled song. Add to this litany a blue-tinged legacy of torch singers peopled by such avatars of dejection as Billie Holiday, Edith Piaf and Jacques Brel, not to mention gloomy latter-day acolytes like Kurt Cobain or Nick Cave, and it becomes clear that Cohen is far from being alone in his much-trumpeted miserablism.

Unsurprisingly, Cohen was inspired as a teenager by the music of figures like Hank Williams, the self-destructive country legend with heartbreak etched into his every crotchet, and Frankie Laine, the impassioned and tearfully love-torn 1950s balladeer. Even his other great musical hero, the jazz/soul/country eminence Ray Charles, is as likely to be heard lamenting his bad luck in the anguished 'Take These Chains From My Heart' as he is revelling in the euphoric 'I Got A Woman'. Almost from the moment that he had ears to listen with, it seems Cohen was drawn to the kind of music with which he would later become synonymous. And it shouldn't be forgotten that even before entering a recording studio Cohen had spent 15 years as a poet and novelist, doing what nearly every poet and novelist does: unburdening himself in verse and prose.

What distinguishes Cohen as the nabob of despondency, then, is not just his penchant for pessimistic navel-gazing. Clearly he was not unique in this regard. Not that such concerns aren't well represented in his work – after all, his reputation as a Canadian literary tyro was based almost entirely on his first collection of poetry, *The Spice-Box Of Earth*, which was, like so much that was to follow, portentous, self-absorbed and shot through with sublimely drawn personal agonies. Similarly, the dualistic dilemma of his simultaneous attraction to both the sacred and the profane occupied him from the moment his fingers first struck the keys of his typewriter. Diligent attention to these inner traumas, moreover, is what led to the early drafts of his first novel, *Beauty At Close Quarters*, being rejected by his publisher Jack McClelland. McClelland's contemporary comments about the author are revealing, describing the book as, 'morbid...very tedious...a protracted love-affair with himself'. Evidence of a contrived, ersatz melancholia perhaps, though these are observations with which any self-dissecting author might be assumed to be familiar.

Nevertheless, accusations of self-pity and an over-abundance of bathos are the price Cohen has paid his entire creative life for repeatedly tearing out his heart and pinning it resolutely to his sleeve. 'Mostly I'm on the front line of my own tiny life', he has said in candid defence of his solipsistic calling.

More significant than such self-centred thematic predispositions, however, more telling, even, than the frequency of his lyrical references to razor blades, ovens and furnaces, or the conflation of piety with lustful viscerality, is the sound of Leonard Cohen. Where contemporary confessors in song from John Lennon to Paul Simon and Bob Dylan laid bare their tortured souls in voices that ranged from the angelic to the idiosyncratic, Cohen essayed his in tones of such grave despair that it could only invite the audience to imagine him permanently on the brink of weeping or, worse, giving up the ghost altogether. Significantly, a non-speaker of English would have no trouble in gauging the general meaning behind a Leonard Cohen song simply from the somnolent timbre of that voice, which, perhaps, goes some way to explaining his instant, enduring and massive appeal across the nations of Europe.

The London *Times*, reviewing Cohen's debut, *Songs Of Leonard Cohen*, in 1968, encapsulated a still enduring reaction to the dire mood of his compositions, comparing him unfavourably with Dylan. 'Whereas Mr. Dylan is alienated from society and mad about it, Mr. Cohen is alienated and merely sad about it'. The same article went on to describe his style as one of 'neo-Keatsy world-weariness'.

In addition to the overweening dourness and the bruised, ponderous pipes, Cohen's preference for stark minor chords and elegiac, hymnal melodies only served to darken an already brooding template. The dolorous thrum of his trademark Spanish guitar and preponderance of glowering cellos that adorn his early albums heighten the desolate mood. His songs often sound like they've been trawled from the dank basement of the soul, whatever the sentiments of the lyrics contained within.

Cohen defended the apparent negativity inherent in his work in 1979: 'There's a confusion between depression and seriousness. I happen to like the mode of seriousness. It's peaceful and relaxing to me to be serious'. Ten years earlier, though, he was more willing to emphasise the potency of personal pain. 'Suffering has led me to where I am. Suffering has made me rebel against my own weakness.'

In his study *Mourning and Melancholia*, Sigmund Freud describes the nature of the truly melancholic in some detail. 'The distinguishing features are a profoundly painful dejection, cessation of interest in all the outside world, loss of capacity to love, inhibition of all activity and a lowering of the self-regarding feelings.' Cohen's 'capacity to love' has never been in doubt, he can normally be relied upon to send his many works out into the world, even if their births are often slow and tortuous, and his activities can rarely be described as 'inhibited'. Serious, not melancholic, it is, then.

Likewise, he has always been frank about the limitations of his vocal instrument. 'I can't stand it most of the time,' he said when asked about his dismal inflections in 1972, before his voice truly deepened. 'There are some people who don't think I've got a golden voice,' he remarked wryly, sixteen years later, alluding to the self-referential line in *Tower Of Song*. In 1967 Cohen was so uncertain about the effectiveness of his singing voice that he told Marty Machat that he was unable to go on playing in front of live audiences; to which the laconic lawyer replied, 'None of you guys can sing. When I want to hear singers I go to the Metropolitan Opera.'

If Cohen is the byword for suicidal tendencies in music, then, it's a combination of his less-than-dulcet larynx, sepulchral musical arrangements and florid lyrics bent on occasionally nihilistic profundity that is to blame. Somehow the sum of these elements adds up to a greater, darker whole when executed by the dapper, middle-class Canadian with the impeccable manners and the Greek island summer home. For Cohen's blues are, indubitably, the bourgeois blues. It is this, perhaps above all, that arouses the suspicion of the cynics and detractors and the empathy of his (generally educated, middle-class) celebrants. If someone from such a comfortable background is so miserable, the thinking goes, then he must be really miserable.

Reaction to Cohen's first musical epistles did not dwell exclusively on the man's glum disposition, nor on his self-indulgence. Many greeted his early forays in quite another way. Reviewing *Songs Of Leonard Cohen*, the English music paper *Sounds* eulogised that it was 'probably the most beautiful album that anyone could own'. The paper's readers obviously agreed, sending the album to Number 2 in the national charts.

By 1974, Cohen was a seasoned debunker of his pessimistic reputation. 'I received a letter from a girl in a German city and it was one of the most touching things that I have ever read. It was about her friend who had died of cancer and who listened to my songs over and over for comfort. Perhaps the songs have a form or a mood that is melancholy but they are not meant to depress. On the contrary, I know that in some cases they can have the opposite effect.'

As is still very much the case, his critics have always been matched, if not outweighed, by disciples entranced by the man's sensitivity and wit, for whom a lamenting minor-key dirge is as likely to be a thing of transcendent beauty as a torpid trial. And in the musical hothouse of the late 1960s, where The Beatles' experimental exotica was nurturing green shoots that would manifest themselves as bombastic progressive rock on one hand and frivolous glam rock on another, Cohen was brave and self-assured enough to cast a considered, even esoteric shadow across the riotous blooms. It is easy to forget that his biggest-selling albums, the first three, were the same ones being regularly dismissed by critics as unengaging studies in alienation. But Cohen always had allies who were touched by his music enough to regard him as an unlikely figurehead. In 1972 an American journalist voiced the opinion that Cohen was 'unquestionably Canada's most important pop cultural icon.' Not bad for a country that had supplied Neil Young, The Band and Joni Mitchell.

Cohen's legacy in the annals of popular song is one of rigour and even sobriety in a milieu predicated upon transient thrills and instant hits. For all his dalliances with the superficiality of the pop world (particularly his collaborations with Phil Spector and Elton John), Cohen's is a literary, high-art calling, music being merely a vehicle for expressing the interior landscape of the poetic mind. In this regard Cohen is greatly indebted to Bob Dylan.

Dylan's ground-breaking and meteoric evolution from early-'60s protest singer to iconic amphetamine poet and seriously bearded late-'60s shaman set a precedent which many a singer-songwriter followed. Dylan opened the floodgates for poetry and experiment in rock music. Without him The Beatles would have gone on billing and cooing about holding hands, while artists as diverse as Van Morrison and David Bowie might never have had their subsequent careers without Dylan's precedent. Dylan legitimised intimate, elaborate, and sometimes pretentious lyrical flights in the context of popular music.

Cohen is no exception to the liberating effect of Dylan's pioneering efforts – as he freely admits. 'When I saw what Dylan had done, it wasn't so much the material, although one was staggered by the excellence of the material, but I'd already published several books, I'd already refined in some way that lyrical gift. So I wasn't influenced in the sense I want to write songs, the songs that Dylan wrote, but his position, his role touched me very deeply. He was the boy come out of the mist.' Dylan himself repaid the compliment, being a regular attendant at Cohen's early-'70s shows and later covering 'Hallelujah' and likening it and other Cohen songs to prayers.

But while Dylan's odyssey took him on a meandering path from callow troubadour to evangelical gospel singer and gypsy traveller-cum-nightly entertainer, Cohen stayed true to his calling throughout his half-century of writing and performing. His concerns emblazoned across the stanzas of *The Spice-Box Of Earth* and *Beautiful Losers* were echoed in the lyrics of *Songs Of Leonard Cohen*, reiterated in *Songs From A Room* and *Songs Of Love & Hate*, expanded in *New Skin For The Old Ceremony* and *Recent Songs*, then further developed in *Various Positions*, *I'm Your Man* and *The Future*.

Some may argue that if Cohen was as true to his art as his supporters claim him to be, then he should never have ventured into the world of popular music at all. Surely, the argument goes, an artist given to literary conceits ought to operate in a strictly literary world? That Cohen spent 15 years doing just that, winning many accolades and becoming a household name in the country of his birth, is often overlooked. Yet the impetus for his discipline-hopping was a desire to, on the one hand, reach a wider audience than the rarefied sphere of the literary cognoscenti and, on the other, finally to make a decent living from his writings. This more than anything crystallizes the paradoxical nature of Cohen's creative life, characterised as it is by the twin motivations of exploration and security.

Cohen always defends himself against accusations of ruthlessly ambitious bandwagon-jumping with regards to his musical career. 'Poetry is no substitute for survival,' he admitted when asked why he turned to songwriting. 'In hindsight,' he went on, stressing the perilous nature of his decision, 'it seems like a very foolish strategy, but I said to myself, I am a country musician...I have songs and this is the way I'm going to address the economic crisis. It seems mad.' More tellingly he points out the similarity between the two disciplines.

'(Literary) writing grew out of my interest in folk music. I never really separated the two activities, writing and music. I've always felt there was an invisible guitar behind the prose writing I've done and even the verse I've done.'

And while Cohen's themes have been intimate, spiritual and couched in intricate, often arcane, language, his music is constructed from the simplest two- or three-chord structures. 'When I have my guitar in my hand, I can just, like, hit the chord of A major and the mood just falls right out, all over the place,' he confesses, hinting at being shackled to his métier.

If the musical skeleton is a basic one then the marriage between it and Cohen's finely-wrought lyrics is what gives the man's trademark comi-tragic style its poignancy and naturalness. Not that such apparent effortlessness is in any way the product of indolently accepted happenstance or serendipity. On the contrary, songwriting for Cohen is a painstaking process, with many hours, days and sometimes years devoted to the intense sculpting of chords, the considered teasing of themes, the diligent pursuit of the *mot juste*. He has only envy for those, Bob Dylan amongst them, who seem able to pluck a song, fully formed, from the ether. At a Paris café meeting in 1985, Dylan enquired of Cohen how long it took him to write the song 'Hallelujah'. 'Five months,' was Cohen's reply (he was being coy – it actually took nearer 18). In response Cohen asked Dylan how long it had taken him to pen the song 'I And I' from his *Infidels* album, with which Cohen was much taken, to which Dylan replied, 'about five minutes.'

There has only been one real instance of Cohen completing a song at one sitting: 'Sisters Of Mercy'. He recalls the romantic, filmic-sounding circumstances: 'I was in Edmonton, doing a tour, by myself, of Canada. I guess this was around '67, and

I was walking along one of the main streets of Edmonton. It was bitter cold and I knew no one and I passed these two girls in a doorway. They invited me to stand in the doorway with them. Of course I did, and sometime later we found ourselves in my little hotel room, in Edmonton, and the three of us were going to go to sleep together. Of course I had all sorts of erotic fantasies about what the evening might bring. We went to bed together and I think we all jammed into this one small couch in this little hotel and it became clear that that wasn't the purpose of the evening at all, and at one point in the night I found myself unable to sleep. I got up and by the moonlight, it was very, very bright, and the moon was being reflected off the snow and my windows were very light and I wrote that poem by the ice-reflected moonlight while these women were sleeping, and it was one of the few songs I ever wrote from top to bottom without a line of revision. The words flowed and the melody flowed and by the time they woke up the next morning, it was done, I had this completed song to sing to them.'

That Cohen is generally more assiduous about his song-writing is plain to see. His albums are few and far between, just ten (including two live recapitulations) in thirty years; so that which does appear carries a greater weight of expectancy than might otherwise be the case. Time is always a factor in the construction of his songs, as he is loath to accede. 'It's an ordeal. Some people write effortlessly. Thomas Wolfe wrote 40,000 words a night on top of his refrigerator and people write peerless songs in the back of taxi cabs. I've been waiting for these graceful moments but they never arrive.'

One reason why Cohen has been criticised for the homogeneity of his songs and their lyrical concerns is that the elongated gaps between albums invite the audience to imagine the man exploring virginal territories, which, of course, he rarely does. And while his musical palette has become broader in his later years, the overriding leitmotifs of love, lust and spiritual yearning are ever-present throughout his 100-song oeuvre.

If it isn't the atmosphere of abject gloom, the paucity of new lyrical subjects, the suspicion that his is a pseudo-poetry, or just his vocal idiosyncrasies that ignite the ire of the anti-Cohenists, then it is his attitude toward women that really gets their goat.

An intense devotee of womankind since adolescence, Cohen's proclivities for the opposite sex are part and parcel of his personal mythology. If he is disconsolate in song then his misery is about a woman; if he is priapic and voyeuristic then it is a woman's intimacy he craves, and if he is an evocative weaver of images, then it is a woman he is attempting to seduce with his alluring language. Or so the image of Cohen that has become the accepted stereotype would have it. Not that he is guiltless with regard to the fuelling of this perception. His dealings with women are decidedly un-politically correct, certainly not in the sense that we understand the parameters of inter-gender behaviour at the turn of the 21st century. Cohen's stance is decidedly mid-20th century in this regard. Seeing women as potential conquests on one hand and as nourishing muses on the other, is, on the surface, a romantic conceit worthy of the novelist Henry Miller. But whereas the American erotic writer saw his libidinous creative life as a speeding rollercoaster of fleeting sexual liaisons, Cohen's lustfulness was constantly battling against the opposite pull of romantic love and cloistered coupledom.

Despite his serial womanising, Cohen spent over 15 years embroiled in just two significant relationships and has always acted with the petulance of an intensely jealous teenager if one or other of his paramours so much as hinted at the roguish behaviour to which he himself was so abjectly prone.

Nevertheless, Cohen is ready to admit his weaknesses with disarming candour, and tries to distance himself from the picaresque life prescribed by Henry Miller and other questing, bohemian Don Juans. 'I was obsessed with gaining women's favours at a certain point in my life and way beyond any reasonable activity. It became the most important thing in my life and it led into very excessive behaviour and some very interesting things. Probably most of the things that I learned about myself and about other people were gained from this period of obsessive...or this blue movie I threw myself into. But we know that blue movies are not romantic.'

But his investment in the redemptive ecstasy of love is still his *raison d'être*, as this more recent statement attests: 'In the sweaty, passionate, filthy embrace, in all of its delicious and time-solving power, in the midst of that embrace there is no difference, no separation between the spiritual and the profane.'

In his later years Cohen has taken on an inevitably different persona. No longer even the crinkled roué, he is pragmatic about his waning appetites and seems bent on attaining the dignity his youthful behaviour eschewed. 'Growing old is the only game in town,' he told a Los Angeles reporter in 1997, 'but it puts you off a lot of the other games you've become attached to, like romance, because there's nothing more inappropriate than seeing an old guy coming on.'

Cohen's other great thirst in life is for spiritual fulfilment, a need expressed by his devotion to the parables and lessons of the Bible, to his Jewish heritage and, perhaps most keenly given recent developments, his adherence to the teachings of Zen Buddhism.

When he was a child, Cohen's mother would often remind her son that his ancestors were the wise and spiritually enlightened members of the community (Cohen means 'priest' in Hebrew). He seems to have taken this information very much to heart, to the extent that much of his life has been spent with his nose in the scriptures, whether they be Hebrew, Christian or Eastern, and has conducted his creativity in the form of a meditation, a search for metaphysical meaning, whatever the implications of his more earth-bound predilections.

With such early familial influences embedding themselves deep in the Cohen psyche, it is perhaps unsurprising that spirituality has been an ever-present theme in both his public career and in his myriad solitary moments.

Cohen's recent compositions may well be, as Bob Dylan so shrewdly observed, 'like prayers', but the truth is that Cohen's songs have been painted with a Judaeo-ecclesiastical patina throughout his musical evolution. Across the panoply of his hundred songs, from 'Story Of Isaac' to 'Anthem', via 'Who By Fire' and 'The Law', there are many more direct examples of his use of the nominally religious form. Cohen explained his fascination with vehemently-held religious beliefs in a 1974 interview: 'Religious fanatics, I find, are extremely good company. They seem to have very specific views and they seem to be in a state of attractive nervousness the whole time.' He elaborated on the theme in a later interview: 'those churches, those mosques, those synagogues, they give comfort and solace to millions and millions of people. I don't think it serves anything or anybody to become an enemy of organised religion.'

Cohen's interest in religious matters also focuses on ritualistic and ephemeral elements. His adolescent enchantment with the sophisticated verse of the Old Testament has never left him and, even as the tenure of his writings has become less grave and more earthbound, within them the sacred still manages to share living space with the secular. Consider the pay-off verse to 'Light As The Breeze', the last Cohen composition on his most recent studio album, 1992's *The Future*, a droll but simple enough song, easily understood as a homage to a lifetime enjoying the intimate, female-pleasuring delights of cunnilingus. Not much room for God in that scenario, you might reasonably conclude. But Cohen is a master of the incongruous juxtaposition and the song, true to form, ends with the following lines, 'So I knelt there at the altar of the alpha and the omega, I knelt there like one who believes/And like a blessing come from heaven for something like a second, I was cured and my heart was at ease'.

It is Cohen's ability to locate the redemptive and the spiritually profound within prosaic and sometimes visceral lyrical contexts that gives his work the poignant astringency in which his fans revel and at which his detractors balk. His ability to almost nonchalantly conflate piety with profanity is a facet he is regularly forced to defend: 'I've always found theology a certain kind of delightful titillation,' he told a recent interviewer. 'Theology or religious speculation bears the same relationship to real experience as pornography does to lovemaking. They're not entirely unconnected. I mean, you can get turned on.'

Much as he never found reason to rebel, in the habitual teenage manner, against his parents, so Cohen has never extinguished the flame of religion that was ignited by his family's gently observed Judaism. 'I think that our faith is full of atheists and agnostics. There was something in it for me. I still had to go whoring after false gods, and maybe I'm still in the bed of one (Buddhism), but there was something about what I saw. I grew up in a Catholic city and Catholic friends have horror stories about what Catholicism is, and my Jewish friends have horror stories about what Judaism is. I never had them, I always thought it was great and I've tried to keep it up in my own half-assed way.'

Musically, Cohen can't, it seems, help but imply a sense of sacramental gravity. There is something of the mournful lamenting of the East European Jewish tradition in his songs, a tradition his mother had passed on to her musically receptive son. Cohen once described his style as 'country and eastern', and it is that solemn, invocatory flavour that pervades the majority of his oeuvre.

At the same time his lyrics, not content with biblical form and plentiful references to religious iconography and ritual, invoke the actual vocabulary of theological texts (the Jewish Torah, or 'book of laws', as well as the Bible and Buddhist scriptures) to attach a timeless, if not ancient, significance to his lyrical themes. This was the man, after all, whose 1984 publication *The Book Of Mercy* was not, as one might have supposed, a collection of poems, but in fact a formal collection of psalms.

Cohen carries this rarefied language into other areas of lyrical concern, the awed deference to loaded symbols seeping into the most intimate discourse. His songs, for example, often dwell on the metaphor of the heart. Although commonly used as a poetic (and everyday) device for articulating the feelings of romantic love, in Cohen's writing 'heart' takes on a far grander meaning. In Hebrew the word has a specific resonance, referring to the centre of a person's being rather than simply the nexus of emotion. Cohen uses this sense to encapsulate the twin ideas of love – the romantic and the spiritual. A song he is reported to be still working on contains a line about him 'opening his heart like a lily to the heat', as he finds peace of mind atop snowy Mount Baldy.

It is this arcane use of language and image which is the touchstone for Cohen devotees. For this is a rare, visionary poetic stance to plant at the core of a slowly unfurling folk song; a self-aggrandising and pretentious conceit to the castigators, an awe-inspiring bid for the sublime to the fans. Cohen's place in the 'Tower Of Song' is assured as much by his adherence to these timeless lyrical forms as it is by his elegiac dolefulness and epoch-defining troubadour's odyssey.

The bid for the sublime, for some kind of everyday enlightenment or transcendence, as much as the basic urge for tranquility of mind, is what led Cohen to Zen Buddhism. He has always steered clear of becoming a Zen evangelist, instead concentrating on the personal benefits gained in his specific case and pointing out the singular importance of his spiritual guru and drinking buddy, Roshi. 'He happens to be a Zen teacher, but if he was teaching physics in Heidelberg I would study physics in Heidelberg,' he has said. Reinforcing his point, he goes on, 'My teacher never invited me to become a Buddhist. He taught me to distinguish between Remy-Martin and Courvoisier.'

In Zen Buddhism, Cohen initially sought refuge, a way out of depression and an antidote to feelings of existential futility. At 66 he has given his life and time (and money – he has been quietly raising funds for Roshi since the 1970s) to the religion that has helped remove the obstacles of self-doubt and self-loathing that have afflicted him even during the phases of his greatest success. But Cohen remains circumspect in his old age. 'It's dangerous if you think Zen exists as salvation. Look at it that way then you're just going to get yourself into a religion that is especially rigorous, while you have perfectly good religions that are not so rigorous and severe like Judaism and Christianity. You might just as well join the marines if you're interested in that kind of life.'

The final cementing of Leonard Cohen's place in the popular music hall of fame also came, indirectly, by way of Zen. As personally turbulent and creatively mercurial as the 1970s and early '80s were for him, the stability and phlegmatism that exposure to Roshi's meditative regimes instilled in Cohen led to his later work being infused with a warmth, generosity of spirit and sardonic, self-aware lightness that his earlier work only rarely hinted at. He no longer appears to be revelling in his own portent. In 1994 Cohen summarised the change in his attitude. 'Nowadays my only need is to jot everything down. I don't feel that I am a singer, or a writer. I'm just the voice, a living diary.' He went on to explain the benefits of the Zen life with starkly undramatic pragmatism. 'Zen has a kind of empty quality. There is no playful worship. There's no supplication, no dogma, there's no theology. I can't even locate what they're talking about half the time. But it does give you an opportunity, a kind of version of Hemingway's *A Clean Well-Lighted Place*. It gives you a place to sit that is quiet in which you can work these matters out.'

And work them out he has. His records show the progression. From *Various Positions*, where the previously black self-portraiture is replaced by a fatalistic self-mocking ('I'll go down to Bill's Bar, I can make it that far,' from 'Night Comes On'), to *The Future*, where admittedly dystopian visions are leavened with similarly playful insights ('We're drinking and we're dancing but there's nothing really happening/The place is dead as Heaven on a Saturday night,' from 'Closing Time'), the change in atmosphere is palpable.

Most emblematic of all in this regard is the album *I'm Your Man*. While *Various Positions* ushered in a new Leonard Cohen, *I'm Your Man*, its follow-up, trumpeted a wry new persona with such refreshing aplomb that it reacquainted his music with the pop charts of the world (if not the USA) and propelled him back to a level of celebrity he hadn't enjoyed since the close of the 1960s. The album was a masterstroke in that it combined elements of the old stereotype – the wistful, broken-hearted poesy, the wise but cracked countenance, the aching, ethereal mien, with a new-found line in laconic *weltschmerz* – one that was unavoidably endearing. Somehow the solipsistic, miscreant saint of hopelessness had transformed into an avuncular elder statesman, a crinkle-eyed, pin-striped avatar of the 20th-century blues.

For young musicians of the late 1980s, themselves adrift in a complex sea of disparate genres, an unfocused morass of indie-rock, embryonic grunge, hedonistic dance and plastic pop styles, Cohen's audacious renaissance was a blast of fresh air.

In many ways, Cohen's surrender to the possibilities of the modern recording studio, a surrender that made *I'm Your Man* slick and contemporary but, simultaneously, powerful and resonant, gave his previously monochrome image a luminescent paint-job. That a figure so inextricably linked with the golden age of the singer-songwriter was back, in confident, even effulgent voice, happily re-casting his métier with knowing alacrity, was as uplifting as it was jaw-dropping. For the first time in many years, Cohen's music was ahead of the game, and as a result the wider rock world couldn't help but sit up and take notice.

The tribute albums, particularly the alternative rock-based *I'm Your Fan*, did much to reposition thinking about the phenomenon of Leonard Cohen. No longer the shadowy 1960s *poète maudit* gathering dust at the back of serious record collections, but a vital, timeless beacon in the constellation of influential songwriters, up there with Dylan, Lou Reed, Brian Wilson and Tom Waits as a hip pop stylist; with the *chutzpah* to re-emerge with a new sound and a renewed relevance.

That many of the tribute interpretations of his finest works were essayed with either the old school Cohenesque grimness (Nick Cave & The Bad Seeds' crudely Gothic destruction of 'Tower Of Song' was typical) or emotion-free perfunctoriness (Lloyd Cole foolishly confessed to choosing 'Chelsea Hotel' 'because the chords were the easiest'), further reinforced Cohen's oft-overlooked élan as a performer and inhabitor of his songs. Like *I'm Your Fan*, the more mainstream *Tower Of Song* only pointed up the prototype's deftness and efficacy in remodelling his craft, as Elton John, Suzanne Vega, Bono et al did their best to obliterate every last nuance of emotion in Cohen's repertoire with the same devices (pristine digital sounds and deluxe mixing consoles) with which he himself was ineffably able to make those emotions fresh and pertinent.

True to form, Cohen responded to the tribute records with a mixture of polite gratitude and thinly disguised, wittily voiced ambivalence. Of *I'm Your Fan* he remarked, 'This album was a surprise, a kind of gift. I had nothing to do with the choices of artists or material. Of course I was very touched.' While *Tower Of Song* elicited a similarly pithy reaction: 'I think a number of these covers rank among these artists' best work. They sound truly like themselves doing these songs.'

Reaction to the new Leonard Cohen signalled by *I'm Your Man* and the sell-out world tour which occupied much of 1988 was almost universally positive – another first for an artist whose every previous epistle seems to have invited myriad shades of critical reaction and often one or other brand of controversy. In the three decades in which he had released records, Cohen had never been so patently well-loved.

As a result, his 1988 concerts became an unparalleled blend of religious ceremony and stand-up comedy, with lashings of sacrilegious self-parody further endearing him to the faithful and attracting the favours of a whole new generation of fans keen to see what all the fuss was about.

In England he was dubbed 'Laughing Len' in ironic tribute to the downcast stereotype of old, but also in acknowledgement of a previously unheralded predisposition that now embraced a refined gallows humour and a mature sense of *joie de vivre*. That Cohen now appeared as a smartly besuited regular guy made his a suddenly exotic public image. He was the dark poet turned Los Angeles hipster, the hermitic exile bathing incongruously in the flashbulbs of a Hollywood premiere, the '60s refusenik finally embracing the world and his role within it. The fact that the nihilism and narcissism of old was still hovering between the lines of every song and in the wings of every humorous aside only seemed to heighten the magnetising effect of his newly urbane and dignified personality.

In Cohen-friendly Europe (where even *Various Positions* had enjoyed extended chart success), *I'm Your Man* was received with unremitting rapture. It stayed at the Number 1 spot for an incredible 17 weeks in Norway (threatening the record held by The Beatles) and 14 in Spain. CBS even awarded Cohen a Crystal Globe Award, one reserved for their artists who sell more than 5 million copies of an album in foreign territories. *I'm Your Man* made Leonard Cohen a pop star all over again.

Canadian reaction to Cohen's second coming was fulsome. In March 1991 he received a coveted induction into the Juno Hall Of Fame (the equivalent of the Grammys) and the following October his country honoured him as an Officer Of The Order Of Canada. The citation at his investiture read, 'One of the most popular and influential writers of his generation, whose work has made Canadian literature familiar to readers abroad. Images of beauty, despair, outrage and tenderness are found in his lyrical poetry and prose, whose themes of love, loss and loneliness touch a universal chord in us all.' Noble and profound sentiments that might just as easily be applied to Cohen's musical outpourings which have, after all, propelled his name and influence into far greater spheres than his purely text-based works.

Cohen reacted to the widespread positivity with good grace and acknowledged the shift of emphasis in his writing. Not that the process of song construction was getting any easier for him as a result. In a 1988 interview he blamed the limitations of his voice for his adherence to the strict disciplines of songwriting. 'If I had one of those good voices, I would have done it completely differently,' he confessed. 'I would probably have sung the songs I really like rather than be a writer. I just don't think one would have bothered to write if one could really have lifted one's voice in song. But that wasn't my voice. This is my voice.'

At nearly four years in the writing, *I'm Your Man*'s follow-up, *The Future*, was testament to the precision with which Cohen attends to his craft. Unfortunately some of the momentum from the *I'm Your Man* period was lost in the intervening time. Not that Cohen's popularity had ebbed, exactly –

rather the zeitgeist had moved on and the sound of whirring synthesizers and pulsing sequencers in service of Cohen's distinctive baritone was no longer a surprise. Coupled with that, the same baritone which had guided him into authorship was by now a barely functioning growl. It suited some of the apocalyptic motifs of *The Future* but its by now bruised and unremitting frequencies tended to provoke some of the old criticisms. The tour that accompanied promotion of the album had the critics reaching for their negative lexicons again. The *London Free Press* described his singing as a 'white man drone and mumble', while others pronounced his vocal abilities as variously 'shot', 'ragged', or 'pained'. The *San Francisco Chronicle* went further, detailing his onstage deportment: 'He stood, clenched fists in front of the chest to emphasise whatever meaning the voice left out.'

Despite the privations of the vocal cords and the disenchanted sentiments of the most recent material, enough revision in the critical perception of Cohen had been undertaken to allow the overriding tendency of his reception to be one of support leavened with the odd caveat. His permanent reinstatement as a figure of gravity, dignity and wit seemed to be assured.

It was certainly a good as well as brave career decision to desist from further album-making in the 1990s. His place in the canon of popular music now enshrined and his reputation revived, Cohen's silence only allows his significance to quietly mature, away from the glare of public expectation. Well into his seventh decade, it is easy to imagine the finally phlegmatic Cohen gazing out over the Californian landscape from his mountain-top eyrie and looking back on his unique career with an enormous sense of satisfaction.

Of course, Cohen being Cohen, such a notion would

probably equate to the kind of negligent entropy he has been fighting to stave off his whole life, hence his insistence on the continuation of his writing and scheming in whatever time his daily meditations allow.

Throughout his creative life Cohen has always been peripatetic. From Montreal to New York, Hydra to Los Angeles, his has been a life of self-imposed exile. His extended visits to London, Paris, Cuba, Ethiopia and Israel only add to this impression. But why was his muse such an itinerant one, what benefit did he gain from adhering so exactly to the stereotype of the wandering Jew? Cohen's own observations about a life of hotels and few possessions are revealing. In 1964 Cohen revealed to a reporter who queried his predilection for living out of a suitcase that 'You always have the feeling in a hotel room that you're on the lam and it's one of the safe moments in the escape. It's a breathing spot. The hotel room is the oasis of downtown. A kind of temple of refuge, sanctuary.' In the same way his protracted sojourns abroad imbued his everyday life with a grand romanticism, as he expounded 20 years later, 'I sometimes in my wilder moments consider myself the leader of a government in exile.'

But there are less frivolous reasons behind his gypsy life, motivations that are inextricably interwoven with the sacrosanct creative process. 'There are two periods in a writer's life,' he surmised in 1974, 'one, the time when he must leave the country in order to get a perspective on his culture, then another time comes when he must go back and renew his contacts with the roots of his culture, otherwise he will become an expatriate writer and he will no longer be nourished by the living language and the living experience of his people.'

For Cohen, then, the further he travels the more certain is his ultimate return. Although he hasn't always been so keen about every aspect of life in his wintry Canadian homeland. 'I shouldn't be in Montreal at all,' he revealed in a 1964 interview, when quizzed about his then ping-pong lifestyle between Hydra and his home town. 'Winter is all wrong for me,' he went on, 'I belong beside the Mediterranean. My ancestors made a terrible mistake. But I have to keep coming back to Montreal to renew my neurotic afflictions.'

Cohen's influence on musicians in his own country is a major one. While his oft-referred-to 'neurotic afflictions' are undoubtedly part and parcel of that influence, the importance of his role is as much about creating a distinctly Canadian voice in rock music as it is a legacy of maudlin, introspective songwriting. Along with Joni Mitchell (and, to a lesser extent, Neil Young), his has been the primary home-grown authorial precedent for Canadian musicians in the 1980s and beyond. Cohen's insistence on trumpeting Canadianism as distinct from Americanism is a major contributory factor in this regard. He has always been quick to differentiate between the two cultures. 'Whatever we call this thing, Canada, it's one of the best places in the world. It's our ambiguities about it that make it great. Those ambiguities about it create all sorts of loopholes where we can operate with a great deal of freedom. I have a very warm feeling about this country,' he summarised in 1985. He has even been known to resort to more specific nationalistic pronouncements about the mother country, as this quote from the same 1985 interview reveals: 'I've lived in Canada most of my life and never felt a great desire to move south of the border' – ironic, since he was living, as he continues to do, in southern California. He went on, 'An artist or a sportsman or a scientist even, has to have the stamp of approval from America before we take him seriously. That's the sad thing. We're just a few cities arranged along the border of the United States, so our sense of identity is continually being threatened.'

Whether it be the self-dissecting psycho-babble of Alanis Morissette, the love-torn melancholia of Sarah McLachlan, the deathly neo-country of Cowboy Junkies or the introverted torch-singing of Mary Margaret O'Hara, Cohen's implicit influence has wound its way through the succeeding generations of Canadian singers and songwriters like a slow reflecting river.

Further afield there is the faux-Biblical introspection of latter-day Nick Cave from Australia, the street stories of New York folk songstrel Suzanne Vega (with whom Cohen maintains a friendship – there's just something about those Suzannes...), Tori Amos's cathartic confessional vignettes, or the visionary yearnings of the late Jeff Buckley (who memorably covered Cohen's 'Hallelujah'), to add to the Cohenesque regiment. More importantly still (and in common with Bob Dylan, Tim Hardin and Tim Buckley, but few others) Cohen's melding of the troubadour folk form with the profoundly autobiographical, spiritually questing motifs of poetry helped establish an entire genre within popular music that has, from Nick Drake to Van Morrison, from Kris Kristofferson to Will Oldham, provided some of the most poignant popular music of the last 30 years.

Without Cohen's precedent certain artists' careers might have been very different. In some cases they might never have existed at all. It's far from inconceivable, for example, that without Cohen's auteurism Kris Kristofferson would have laboured long in the songwriting dens of Nashville's Music Row – the excellence of his 'Me & Bobby McGee' notwithstanding – without ever stepping in front of a microphone himself. Kristofferson's early solo outings – particularly 1971's *The Silver Tongued Devil & I* album – are replete with dark, confessional country balladry that owes more than a passing nod to Cohen. As well as the snail's-pace tempos and understated acoustic settings, Kristofferson's parched baritone voice is a dead ringer for Cohen's. On songs that are only nominally country, like 'Jesus Was A Capricorn' and 'Epitaph' (the latter written for and performed at the funeral of another Cohen affiliate, Janis Joplin), he encompassed Cohen's by turns sardonic world-weariness and ribald religious imagery with a deftness bordering on homage. Cohen was a key constituent of the new wave of folk-rock-based artists which liberated Nashville from the mawkish whimsy of bad puns and conservative stereotypes that had long hamstrung the genre.

Another artist who came to prominence at the same time as Cohen, and was much influenced by his style, was the Cree Indian folk singer Buffy Sainte-Marie (they even wrote a song together, 'God Is Alive, Magic Is Afoot'). Sainte-Marie's natural tendency – a querulous, occasionally yelping vocal delivery, essaying simple songs with, generally, political preoccupations, was memorably mollified on such songs as 'Sometimes When I Get To Thinking' and 'He's A Keeper Of The Fire'. On these downbeat selections from the late 1960s, Sainte-Marie's tone is suddenly less brusque, her lyrics bathed in mysticism one minute, confessional the next. She even wrote a song called 'Winter Boy', surely a bookend to Cohen's own 'Winter Lady'.

As the 1970s unfolded, Cohen's name became a byword for bedsit angst. His model provided *carte blanche* for lonely souls with cheap acoustic guitars to impress their paramours with tortuous poetry essayed in an unrelenting drone over a churning A-minor chord. Through the later half of the 1970s Cohen's specific influence was less tangible. Indeed he was consigned to the ignominy of laughing stock by punk's tyros who readily dismissed him as just another precious, self-indulgent and irrelevant enemy of youthful irreverence. Cohen recalls, 'My name was basically used for comic relief in those days.' Of course he was hoisted back onto the pedestal by the more open-minded generation that held sway in the wake of punk's liberating year zero, as the *I'm Your Fan* tribute attests.

Amongst the swollen ranks of literary-minded, minor chord-worshipping camp followers were several artists – much beloved of rock critics – whose punk-inspired zeal was matched by deference to the singer-songwriter heritage personified by Leonard Cohen. Typical of this strain was Nick Cave. Cave, along with his bands The Birthday Party and The Bad Seeds, represents a paradigm of youthful belligerence transmuting into phlegmatic, urbane and mature songwriting. Where once he revelled in clumsy Gothic imagery and broken-glass guitars, the grown-up Cave, when not unearthing arcane murder ballads, now essays elegantly forlorn laments, dripping in strings and muted pianos, that are characterised by a knowing, subtly self-deprecating wit and a singing voice of dubious musicality. It's possible to hear the Cohenisation of Cave on the aching 'Sad Waters' from 1986's *Your Funeral...My Trial* album, or most tracks on his recent *The Boatman's Call* collection. The B-side of Cave's 1992 single 'Straight To You' includes the song 'Bluebird', surely the greatest Cohen song that Leonard never wrote.

That Cave has written a Biblically-themed novel, two collections of poetry, dabbled in film, had one or two high profile affairs and spent his thirties encased in dark, elegantly-tailored suits just adds to the sense of *déjà vu*. This could all be idle conjecture without the evidence of Cave's galumphing contribution to *I'm Your Fan* and his regular trotting out of other Cohen covers (most regularly 'Avalanche', also record-ed on The Bad Seeds' *From Her To Eternity* LP) in his live shows. Cave even lived in exile (in Sao Paulo, Brazil) with spouse and child for several years and continues a peripatetic existence between London, the USA and his native Australia. Expect the monk's robes any day now...

The tentacles of Cohen's influence continue into some of the most critically acclaimed music of the 1990s and, no doubt, beyond. Even a casual listen to Cowboy Junkies' *Crescent Moon*, The Triffids' *Bury Me Deep In Love*, Tindersticks' *The Not Knowing*, American Music Club's *What The Pillar Of Salt Held Up* or Will Oldham's *New Gypsy*, will reveal various elements of Cohenesque mystery and melancholy bubbling away close to the surface of modern rock alchemy.

Without his precedent, it might be reasonably argued, Nirvana's brutal nihilism (compare the similar lyrical tone of their 'Come As You Are' with that of Cohen's 'Famous Blue Raincoat') or Radiohead's bruised comi-tragedy (compare their 'Karma Police' with Cohen's equally paranoid, if more jolly-sounding, 'Jazz Police') might never have found recep-tive ears. For, if nothing else, Cohen's success has forever legit-imised angst as one of serious rock music's major tenets.

Whether or not Cohen proceeds with his own musical career (he is reported to have been working on several songs throughout his years of seclusion, but to date at least, CBS have nothing Cohen-related scheduled in their release itiner-ary) he can rest assured that his name is carved into the hearts of his millions of fans and stitched resolutely into the very fabric of rock history. And if Cohen never again essays a note of music, his keystone position in the hierarchical architecture of the idiom is assured. He is a heroic figure in Canada and much of Europe, a bewildering cult presence shimmering on the horizon of the American pop experience and for those who have followed, supported and occasionally questioned his half-century of peerless poetic striving, he remains a uniquely enigmatic artistic totem of the second half of the twentieth century.

His friend and mentor the Canadian poet Irving Layton has the final word on the lugubrious force of nature that is Leonard Cohen. 'Leonard is the only man I know who really goes beyond concepts, or ideas. Of him too one could say, as someone said of Yeats, that his mind was never violated by an idea, something like that. He thinks with his whole body and he has recognised somewhere, perhaps in the womb of his mother, that concepts blot out or distort experience and that he wants the living spontaneous, freshness of it. But the point is he lives that way. His whole life is the best argument. He astounds, confounds and finally destroys his opponents by simply being.'

INDEX

PICTURE CREDITS

Picture section page 1: Glenn A. Baker Archives/Redferns. 2 top and bottom: David Redfern/Redferns. 3 top and bottom: Pieter van Acker/Camera Press. 4: Dr. H.J. Dibbert/Redferns. 5: Gems/Redferns. 6 main picture: Ebet Roberts/Redferns; inset: Jane Harbury/Redferns. 7: George Rose/Liaison Agency. 8 top: Gered Mankowitz/Redferns; bottom: Gered Mankowitz/Arena.